THE INTERPRETATION
OF FAIRY TALES

A C.G. JUNG FOUNDATION BOOK

The C. G. Jung Foundation for Analytical Psychology is dedicated to helping men and women to grow in conscious awareness of the psychological realities in themselves and society, find healing and meaning in their lives and greater depth in their relationships, and to live in response to their discovered sense of purpose. It welcomes the public to attend its lectures, seminars, films, symposia, and workshops and offers a wide selection of books for sale through its bookstore. The Foundation also publishes *Quadrant,* a semiannual journal, and books on Analytical Psychology and related subjects. For information about Foundation programs or membership, please write to the C. G. Jung Foundation, 28 East 39th Street, New York, NY 10016.

THE
INTERPRETATION
OF FAIRY TALES

REVISED EDITION

Marie-Louise von Franz

SHAMBHALA
Boulder
1996

Shambhala Publications, Inc.
4720 Walnut Street
Boulder, Colorado 80301
www.shambhala.com

20   19   18   17   16   15   14

Printed in the United States of America

♾ This edition is printed on acid-free paper that meets
the American National Standards Institute Z39.48 Standard.
♻ Shambhala Publications makes every effort to print on recycled
paper. For more information please visit www.shambhala.com.
Distributed in the United States by Penguin Random House LLC
and in Canada by Random House of Canada Ltd

Library of Congress Cataloging-in-Publication Data

Franz, Marie-Louise von, 1915–
The interpretation of fairy tales / Marie-Louise von Franz.—
Rev. ed., 1st ed.
p.   cm.
"A C. G. Jung Foundation book"—
Rev. ed. of: An introduction to the interpretation of fairy tales.
1987 printing, © 1970.
Includes bibliographical references (p.   ) and index.
ISBN 978-0-87773-526-7 (alk. paper)
1. Fairy tales—History and criticism.   2. Psychoanalysis and
folklore.   I. Franz, Marie-Louise von, 1915–   Introduction to the
interpretation of fairy tales.   II. Title.
GR550.F714   1996   95-25815
398′.09—dc20   CIP

CONTENTS

PREFACE

This book resulted from lectures which I gave in English at the C. G. Jung Institute more than twenty years ago. Based upon a recording of the lectures, it was first published in English in 1970.

In these lectures, I summarized for the students the experience I had gained through my contributions of interpretation to the work of Hedwig von Beit in *Symbolik des Märchens*. Apart from some early studies from the Freudian school, as well as some short essays by Alfons Maeder, Franz Riklin, and Wilhelm Laiblin, no interpretations of fairy tales had been published by Jungian authors at that time. That is why it was my primary intention to open up the archetypal dimension of fairy tales to the students. For this reason, the ethnological and folkloristic aspects are only touched upon, which is not meant to imply, however, that I view them as unimportant.

Since then, there has been a real blossoming of fairy tale interpretation from the standpoint of depth psychology. From the Freudian school, primarily Bruno Bettelheim's book *The Uses of Enchantment: The Meaning and Importance of Fairy Tales* should be mentioned. From the Jungian school, so many books have been published that I cannot name them all here. Although it is not my intention to assail colleagues by name, I would nevertheless like to express a very personal opinion here. In many so-called Jungian attempts at interpretation, one can see a regression to a very personalistic approach. The interpreters judge the hero or heroine to be a normal human ego and his misfortunes to be an image of his neurosis. Because it is natural for a person listening to a fairy tale to identify with the main character, this kind of interpretation is understandable. But such interpreters ignore what Max Lüthi found to be essential for magical fairy tales, namely, that in contrast to the heroes of adventurous sagas, the heroes or heroines of fairy tales are abstractions—that is, in our language, archetypes. Therefore, their fates are not neurotic complications, but rather are expressions of the difficulties and dangers given to us by nature. In a personalistic interpretation, the very healing element of an archetypal narrative is nullified.

For example, the hero-child is nearly always abandoned in fairy tales. If one then interprets his fate as the neurosis of an abandoned child, one ascribes it to the neurotic family novel of our time. If, however, one leaves it embedded within its archetypal context, then it takes on a much deeper meaning, namely that the new God of our time is always to be found in the ignored and deeply unconscious corner of the psyche (the birth of Christ in a stable). If an individual has got to suffer a neurosis as a result of being an abandoned child, he or she is called upon to turn toward the abandoned God within but not to identify with his suffering.

Hans Giehrl, in *Volksmärchen und Tiefenpsychologie,* makes what I view to be a partially justified reproach of depth-psychology interpreters, namely that they transfer their own subjective problems onto the fairy tales, where they are not to be found at all. As in all scientific work, the subjective factor can never be entirely excluded. But I believe that by using the basic tool of mythological amplification, one can hold in check such subjectivism and, to some extent, thereby reach a generally valid interpretation.

Another tool we can use to reach a certain level of objectivity is to take the context into consideration. Here, too, Giehrl expresses criticism, though in this respect I do not agree with him. He believes that because variations sometimes include contrary motifs and for this reason are omitted, the objectivity of contextual research is impaired. But if one goes into this more deeply, then one can see that each contrary motif changes the whole context and therefore proves just the opposite. The Russian fairytale "Beautiful Vassilissa" tells the story of a girl's encounter with an ancient witch, which ends on a positive note. The German version, "Frau Trude," ends on a negative note. If one scrutinizes both versions, then one sees that the girl in the Russian version is kind and obedient and has good common sense, whereas her counterpart in the German version is disobedient, impertinent, and cheeky. This permeates the whole context, and because of this, one cannot interpret both fairy tales in the same way, despite the fact that both stories circle around the same archetype of an encounter with the Great Mother.

In what follows, my efforts are aimed at interpreting only a few classical stories, or basic types of important fairy tale plots, as it were, in order to help clarify for the reader the Jungian method of interpretation, a method which I believe to be well substantiated. If, as a result, some readers feel motivated to try their hand at interpretation and have fun doing so, then the goal of this book will have been achieved.

MARIE-LOUISE VON FRANZ
Küsnacht, Switzerland
April 1995

ACKNOWLEDGMENTS

I wish to thank the many people who helped to see this seminar into print: Una Thomas for her faithful transcript, on which the text is based; Marian Bayes and Andrea Dykes for their help with my English; and Thayer Greene for helping to finance the original publication. I would also like to thank Patricia Berry and Valerie Donleavy for the first form in which this seminar appeared.

I also want to thank Mrs. Alison Kappes for translating the additions made in the German version for this new revised English edition. My greatest gratitude goes to Dr. Vivienne Mackrell for helping me to organize this book but mainly for her general support.

THE INTERPRETATION
OF FAIRY TALES

1

THEORIES OF FAIRY TALES

Fairy tales are the purest and simplest expression of collective unconscious psychic processes. Therefore their value for the scientific investigation of the unconscious exceeds that of all other material. They represent the archetypes in their simplest, barest, and most concise form. In this pure form, the archetypal images afford us the best clues to the understanding of the processes going on in the collective psyche. In myths or legends, or any other more elaborate mythological material, we get at the basic patterns of the human psyche through an overlay of cultural material. But in fairy tales there is much less specific conscious cultural material, and therefore they mirror the basic patterns of the psyche more clearly.

In terms of Jung's concept, every archetype is in its essence an *unknown* psychic factor, and therefore there is no possibility of translating its content into intellectual terms. The best we can do is to circumscribe it on the basis of our own psychological experience and from comparative studies, bringing up into light, as it were, the whole net of associations in which the archetypal images are enmeshed. The fairy tale itself is its own best explanation; that is, its meaning is contained in the totality of its motifs connected by the thread of the story. The unconscious is, metaphorically speaking, in the same position as one who has had an original vision or experience and wishes to share it. Since it is an event that has never been conceptually formulated, he is at a loss for means of expression. When a person is in that position he makes several attempts to convey the thing and tries to evoke, by intuitive appeal and analogy to familiar material, some response in his listeners, and never tires of expounding his vision until he feels they have some sense of the content. In the same way we can put forward the hypothesis that every fairy tale is a relatively closed system compounding one essential psychological meaning, which is expressed in a series of symbolic pictures and events and is discoverable in these.

After working for many years in this field, I have come to the conclusion that all fairy tales endeavor to describe one and the same psychic fact, but a fact so complex and far-reaching and so difficult for us to realize in all its different aspects that hundreds of tales and thousands of repetitions with a musician's variations are needed until this unknown fact is delivered into consciousness; and even then the theme is not exhausted. This unknown fact is what Jung calls the Self, which is the psychic totality of an individual and also, paradoxically, the regulating center of the collective unconscious. Every individual and every nation has its own modes of experiencing this psychic reality.

Different fairy tales give average pictures of different phases of this experience. They sometimes dwell more on the beginning stages, which deal with the experience of the shadow and give only a short sketch of what comes later. Other tales emphasize the experience of animus and anima and of the father and mother images behind them and gloss over the preceding shadow problem and what follows. Others emphasize the motif of the inaccessible or unobtainable treasure and the central experiences. There is no difference of value between these tales, because in the archetypal world there are no gradations of value, for the reason that every archetype is in its essence only one aspect of the collective unconscious, as well as always representing also the whole collective unconscious.

Every archetype is a relatively closed energetic system, the energetic stream of which runs through all aspects of the collective unconscious. An archetypal image is not to be thought of as merely a static image, for it is always at the same time a complete typical process including other images in a specific way. An archetype is a specific psychic impulse, producing its effect like a single ray of radiation, and at the same time a whole magnetic field expanding in all directions. Thus the stream of psychic energy of a "system," an archetype, actually runs through all other archetypes as well. Therefore, although we have to recognize the indefinable vagueness of an archetypal image, we must discipline ourselves to chisel sharp outlines which throw the different aspects into bold relief. We must get as close as possible to the specific, determinate, "just so" character of each image and try to express the very specific character of the psychic situation which is contained in it.

Before I try to explain the specific Jungian form of interpretation, I will briefly go into the history of the science of fairy tales and into the theories of the different schools and their literature. We read in Plato's writings that old women told their children symbolic stories—*mythoi*. Even then fairy tales were connected with the education of children. In later antiquity Apuleius, a philosopher and writer of the second century, built into his famous novel *The Golden Ass* a fairy tale called "Amor and Psyche," a type of "Beauty and the Beast" story.[1] This fairy tale runs on the same pattern as those one can nowadays still collect in Norway, Sweden, Russia, and many other countries. It has therefore been concluded that at least this type of fairy tale (that of a woman redeeming an animal lover) has existed for two thousand years, practically unaltered. But we have even older information, because fairy tales have also been found in Egyptian *papyri* and *stelai,* one of the most famous being that of the two brothers Anup (Anubis) and Bata. It runs absolutely parallel to the two brother-type tales, which one can still collect in all European countries. We have written tradition for three thousand years, and what is striking is that *the basic motifs have not changed much.* Furthermore, according to Father Max Schmidt's theory, *Der Ursprung der Gottesidee,* we have information to the effect that certain themes of tales go as far back as twenty-five thousand years before Christ, practically unaltered.[2]

Until the seventeenth and eighteenth centuries, fairy tales were—as they still are in remote primitive centers of civilization—told to adults as well as to children. In Europe they used to be the chief form of wintertime entertainment. In agricultural populations, telling fairy tales became a kind of essential, spiritual occupation. Sometimes it is said that fairy tales represent the philosophy of the spinning wheel *(Rockenphilosophie).*

Scientific interest in them began in the eighteenth century with Winckelmann, Hamann, and J. G. Herder. Others, like K. Ph. Moritz, gave these tales a poetical interpretation. Herder said that such tales contained the remnants of an old, long-buried faith expressed in symbols. In that thought one sees an emotional impulse—the neopaganism which began to stir in Germany as early as the time of Herder's philosophy and which appeared in a very unpleasant way not long ago. Dissatisfaction with Christian teaching and the first longings for a more vital, earthy, and instinctual wisdom began then; later we find it more explicitly among the Romanticists in Germany.

It was this religious search for something which seemed lacking in official Christian teaching that first induced the famous brothers Jakob and Wilhelm Grimm to collect folktales. Before then, fairy tales suffered the same fate as the unconscious itself, which was taken for granted. People take it for granted and live on it, but do not want to admit its existence. They make use of it—for instance, in magic and talismans. If you have a good dream, you exploit it, but at the same time you do not take it seriously. For such people a fairy tale or a dream does not need to be looked at accurately but may be distorted; since it is not "scientific" material, one can just as well spin a little around it, and one has the right to pick what suits one and to discard the rest.

That same strange unreliable, unscientific, and dishonest attitude has for a long time prevailed toward fairy tales. So I always tell students to look up the original. You can still get editions of the Grimm fairy tales in which some scenes have been omitted and those from other fairy tales inserted. The editor or translator is sometimes impertinent enough to distort the story without taking the trouble to make a footnote. They would not dare do that with the Gilgamesh epic or a text of that kind, but fairy tales seem to provide a free hunting ground where some feel free to take any liberty.

The Brothers Grimm wrote down fairy tales literally, as told by people in their surroundings, but even they could sometimes not resist mixing a few versions, though in a tactful way. They were honest enough to mention it in footnotes or in their letters to Achim von Arnim. But even the Grimms did not yet have that scientific attitude, which modern folklore writers and ethnologists try to have, of taking down a story literally and leaving the holes and paradoxes in it, dreamlike and paradoxical as they may sound.

The collection of fairy tales which the Brothers Grimm published was a tremendous success. There must have been a strong unconscious emotional interest, for like a mushroom growth other editions popped up everywhere. In France, the much older edition of Perrault was revised. In every country people began to make a basic collection of their national fairy tales. At once everybody was struck by the enormous number of recurrent themes. The same theme, in thousands of variations, came up again and again in

French, Russian, Finnish, and Italian collections. With this came again Herder's first emotional interest in the search for the remains of an "old wisdom" or "faith." The Brothers Grimm, for instance, used such similes as "a broken crystal whose fragments you still find scattered in the grass."

Parallel to the Brothers Grimm, the so-called symbolic school, whose main representatives are Chr. C. Heyne, F. Creuzer, and J. G. Görres, came into existence. Their basic idea was that myths were the symbolic expression of deep philosophical realizations and thoughts, and were a mystical teaching of some of the deepest truths about God and the world.[3] Though these investigators had some interesting ideas, their explanations now seem to us too speculative. Then came a more historical and scientific interest, an attempt to answer the question why there were so many recurring motifs. Since at this time there was no hypothesis about a common collective unconscious or a common human psychic structure (although some investigators indirectly pointed to it), a passion arose to find out in which spot the fairy tales originated and the paths of their migration. Theodor Benfey tried to prove that all fairy tale motifs originated in India and had migrated to Europe,[4] while others like Alfred Jensen, H. Winkler, and E. Stucken contended that all fairy tales were of a Babylonian origin and had then spread through Asia Minor and from there to Europe. There were many others who tried to construct such theories. One result was the creation of the folklore center known as the Finnish school, whose first representatives were Kaarle Krohn and Antti Aarne. These two men decided that it was not possible to discover only one country in which fairy tales originated, and they assumed that different tales might have had a different original home country. They made collections of the same types of fairy tales with the idea that of all the "Beauty and the Beast" tales, all the helpful-animal tales, and so on, the best and richest version, the most poetical and well-expressed, would be the original and all others would be derivations. There are still people nowadays who search along the same lines, but the hypothesis, it seems to me, can no longer survive because we can see that in being handed on, fairy tales need not necessarily degenerate but may just as well improve. To my thinking, therefore, the scholars of the Finnish school have given us a useful collection of motifs, but we cannot do much with their deductions. Aarne's main book, *Verzeichnis der Märchentypen,* is now published in English.[5]

At the same time there was a movement led by Max Müller which tried to interpret myths as travesties of natural phenomena such as the sun and its different appearances (solar myth, Frobenius), the moon (lunar myth, P. Ehrenreich), the dawn (Stucken and Gubernatis), the life of vegetation (Mannhardt) and the storm (Adalbert Kuhn).

In the nineteenth century some people were already groping in another direction, and here a man must be mentioned who is rarely remembered, although to my mind he has great merit, and that is Ludwig Laistner, who wrote *Das Rätsel der Sphinx.*[6] His hypothesis was that the basic fairy tale and folktale motifs derive from dreams. But he concentrates chiefly on nightmare motifs. Basically, he is trying to show a connection between recurring typical dreams and folklore motifs, and he cites interesting material to prove his point. Though not with reference to folklore, the ethnologist Karl von der Steinen, at the same time, tried at the end of his book *Voyage to Central Brazil* to explain that most magic and supernatural beliefs of the primitives he had been studying derived from dream experiences, for it is a typical mode of primitive behavior that dream experience is regarded as actual and real experience. For instance, if someone dreams that he was in heaven where he talked to an eagle, he is quite justified in telling this the next morning as a fact, without adding that he dreamt it, and that, according to Von der Steinen, is how such stories originated. Another scholar, Adolf Bastian, had an interesting theory that all basic mythological motifs are, as he called them, "elementary thoughts" of mankind.[7] His hypothesis was that mankind has a store of *Elementargedanken* (elementary thoughts), which do not migrate but are inborn in every individual, and that those thoughts appear in different varieties in India, Babylonia, and even, for instance, in South Sea stories. He called the specific stories *Völkergedanken* (national thoughts). His idea clearly approaches Jung's idea of the archetype and the archetypal image, the archetype being the structural basic disposition to produce a certain mythologem, the specific form in which it takes shape being the archetypal image. The elementary thoughts, according to Bastian, are a hypothetical factor; that is, you never see an elementary thought, but the many national thoughts point to the existence of one basic thought underneath.

Intellectuals are sometimes tempted to view archetypes as philosophical thoughts, a misunderstanding which arises out of the very nature of archetypes. We would disagree with Bastian where he speaks of these motifs as "thoughts." He was a very philosophically minded person, obviously a thinking type, and he even tried to interpret some elementary thoughts by associating them with ideas of Kant and Leibniz. For us, on the contrary, the archetype is not only an "elementary thought" but also an elementary poetical image and fantasy, and an elementary emotion, and even an elementary impulse toward some typical action. So we add to it a whole substructure of feeling, emotion, fantasy, and action, which Bastian did not include in his theory.

The hypothesis of Ludwig Laistner and later of Georg Jakob, who wrote a book on the fairy tale and the dream in much the same way as Laistner,[8] had no success, nor were the suggestions made by Karl von der Steinen accepted. Bastian also was discarded by the general scientific world, which went on more along the line of the English Folklore Society and the Finnish Society of Folklore, and since Antti Aarne's book, mentioned above, an enormous and useful work by Stith Thompson has been produced, entitled *Motif Index of Folk Literature.*[9]

Beside the collecting of parallels, new schools have come into existence, one of which is the so-called literary school. It investigates from a purely literary and formal standpoint the difference between the various types of tale, namely the myth, legend, amusing story, animal story, trickster story, and what one might call the classical fairy tale.[10] This forms a very meritorious study. With the typical method of the literary schools, researchers began to compare the hero of the legend with the type of hero in the classical fairy tale and so on. Interesting results have come to light, and I recommend these works.

Another modern movement consists of a group of ethnologists, archeologists, and specialists in mythology and the comparative history of religion, practically all of whom know Jung and Jungian psychology but try to interpret mythological motifs omitting Jung's hypotheses—and naturally the name of Jung as well—and to make indirect use of Jung's discoveries. They write books with titles such as *The Great Goddess* or *The Threefold Godhead* or *The Hero,* and they do not take as a starting point the human individual and his psychic structure, which has produced these symbols, but they sit in the middle of the archetype, so to speak, and let it amplify itself, poetically and "scientifically."

In mythology there is Julius Schwabe and sometimes Mircea Eliade.[11] There is also Otto Huth, who works on fairy tales in this way, Robert Graves, and in some ways Erich Fromm. That is to name just a few, but there are many more. These people are punished for their unscientific and illegitimate approach because they fall into something that they did not foresee. As soon as one approaches an archetype in this way, everything becomes everything.

If you start with the world tree, you can easily prove that every mythological motif leads to the world tree in the end. If you start with the sun, you can easily prove that everything is finally a solar motif. And so you just get lost in the chaos of interconnections and overlapping meanings which all archetypal images have with one another. If you choose the Great Mother or the world tree or the sun or the underworld or the eye, or something else, as a motif, then you can pile up comparative material forever, but you have completely lost your Archimedean standpoint from which to interpret.

In the last paper he wrote, Jung pointed out that this is a great temptation for the intellectual type because intellectuals overlook the emotional and feeling factor, which is always connected with an archetypal image.[12] An archetypal image is not only a thought pattern (as a thought pattern it is connected with every other thought pattern); it is also an emotional experience—the emotional experience of an individual. Only if it has an emotional and feeling value for an individual is it alive and meaningful. As Jung said, you can collect all the Great Mothers in the world and all the saints and everything else, and what you have gathered means absolutely nothing if you leave out the feeling experience of the individual.

Now that is a difficulty, because our whole academic training tends to discard this factor. In college, especially in the natural sciences, when the teacher shows the class a crystal, girls particularly tend to cry out, "Oh, what a beautiful crystal," and then the teacher says, "We are not now admiring the beauty, but want to analyze the structure of this thing." So you are constantly and habitually trained, from the very beginning, to repress your personal emotional reaction and to train your mind to be what we call objective. Now this is all right as far as it goes. I quite agree with it up to a point, but we cannot do it in psychology in the same way, and that is, as Jung said, the difficult position of psychology as a science, for psychology, in contrast to all the other sciences, cannot afford to overlook feeling. It has to take into consideration the feeling tone and emotional value of outer and inner factors, including the observer's feeling reaction as well. As you know, modern physics does accept the fact that the observer and the theoretical hypothesis he has in his mind, on account of which he builds up the experimental setup, does play a role in the result of his investigation. What is not yet accepted is that the emotional factor in the observer may play a role. But physicists will have to rethink that— for, as Wolfgang Pauli has pointed out, we have no *a priori* reason to reject it. Most certainly we can say that in psychology we *have* to take it into consideration. That is why so many academic scientists call Jungian psychology unscientific, because it takes into consideration a factor which has hitherto been habitually and intentionally excluded from the scientific outlook. But our critics do not see that this is not just a whim of ours, or that it is not because we are still so childish that we cannot repress our personal feeling reactions to the material. We know from conscious scientific insight that these feelings are necessary and belong in the method of psychology, if you want to get at the phenomenon in the right way.

If an individual has an archetypal experience—for instance, an overwhelming dream of an eagle coming in through the window— this is not only a thought pattern about which you can say, "Oh yes, the eagle is a messenger from God, and it was one of Zeus's messengers and of Jupiter's, and in North American mythology the eagle appears as a creator," et cetera. If you do that, it is intellectually quite correct for you amplify the archetype, but you overlook the emotional experience. Why is it an eagle and not a raven and not a fox and not an angel? Mythologically, an angel and an eagle are the same thing: an *angelos,* a winged messenger from heaven, from the beyond, from the Godhead, but for the dreamer it makes a lot of difference if he dreams about an angel and all that it means to him or if he dreams of an eagle with all his positive and negative reactions to the eagle. You cannot just skip the dreamer's emotional reactions, though scientifically Eliade and Huth and Fromm and others will simply say both are messengers from the Beyond. Intellectually it is the same thing, but emotionally there is a difference. Thus you cannot ignore the individual and the whole setup into which such an experience falls.

The representatives of this outlook try to pull all the results of Jungian psychology backward into the old setup of academic thinking and to push aside the most important factor which Jung introduced into the science of myths: namely, *the human basis from which such motifs grow.* But you cannot study plants without studying the soil on which they grow: melons grow best on dunghills and not on sand, and if you are a good gardener, you have a knowledge of the soil as well as of the plants, and in mythology *we* are the soil of the symbolic motifs—we, the individual human beings. This fact cannot be ignored under the pretext that it does not exist, but to exclude it is a terrific temptation for thinking types and intellectuals because doing so fits into their habitual attitude.

Let us take the motif of the tree, for example. Let us assume that I am an investigator who has a tree complex, so I will start with that. Being emotionally fascinated by it, I shall say, "Oh, the sun myth and the tree myth are connected, for in the morning the sun is born in the east out of the tree. There is, for instance, the Christmas tree, and every Christmas the tree gives birth to the new light at the moment of the winter solstice. So all the sun myths are in a way also tree myths. But then the tree is also a mother. You know that in Saxony, even now, it is said that beautiful girls grow under the leaves of trees, and I could show you pictures showing that children come from trees; the souls of unborn children rustle under the leaves, and that is why there are trees in the center of all

German, Austrian, and Swiss villages. The tree is therefore the Great Mother. But the tree is not only the mother of life but also the death mother, because from trees coffins are made, and there are the tree burials. The shamans of circumpolar tribes and people in certain North Canadian tribes are buried in a tree. Probably also the Babylonian Zikkurats and those columns on which the Persians put their dead are also a travesty of the tree. Then, have you ever thought of the tree and the well? Under every tree there is a spring. There is the world-ash Yggdrasil with the Urd well underneath, for instance. I can show you Babylonian seals on which there is a tree underneath the well of life, so that all the motifs of the water of life are really associated with the tree; you put your searchlight onto it, and it just depends on tree mythology. That is quite clear! Everybody sees that. But you can also bring the moon in. As the mother the tree is feminine, but it is also the father because the tree is a phallic symbol; for instance, in the Aztec chronicles the word for the original land where the Aztecs and Mayans emigrated represents a broken-off tree, a kind of tree trunk, and the trunk form is a phallic father-image. There are stories of a woman passing a tree and a seed from the tree entering her womb. Therefore, clearly the tree is a father, and that links up with the tree being the sun, which is a father figure. That is obvious!"

If you have a sun complex, then everything is solar, and if you have a moon complex, everything is lunar.

In the unconscious all archetypes are contaminated with one another. It is as if several photographs were printed one over the other; they cannot be disentangled. This has probably to do with the relative timelessness and spacelessness of the unconscious. It is like a package of representations which are simultaneously present. Only when the conscious mind looks at it is one motif selected, because you put your searchlight onto it, and it just depends on where you direct your searchlight first, for in some way you always get the whole of the collective unconscious. Thus for one scientist the mother is everything, for another everything is vegetation, and for another everything is a solar myth. The amusing thing is that all such intellectuals, when they see the connection—for instance, between the tree and the sun or the coffin—then say, "of course" or "obviously" or "naturally." The tree is *obviously* the mother, for instance. I watch to see where the investigator uses these words. It is temptingly easy because archetypal connections *are* obvious and natural, and so the writer says "naturally" or "obviously" and is sure that all his readers will walk into the same trap. Only the intellectual type gets caught in this trap. Others after a while revolt, realizing that it is not possible for everything to be everything else, and they return to the emotional value in difference between symbols.

Actually you can interpret a myth or fairy tale with any of the four functions of consciousness. The thinking type will point out the structure and the way in which all the motifs connect. The feeling type will put them in a value order (a hierarchy of values), which is also completely rational. With the feeling function a good and complete fairy tale interpretation can be made. The sensation type will just look at the symbols and amplify them. The intuitive will see the whole package in its oneness, so to speak; he will be most gifted in showing that the whole fairy tale is not a discursive story but is really *one* message, split up into many facets. The more you have differentiated your functions, the better you can interpret because you must circumambulate a story as much as possible with all four functions. The more you have developed and obtained the use of more conscious functions, the better and the more colorful your interpretation will be. It is an art which has to be practiced. It cannot be learned—apart from some general indications, which I will try to give. I always tell students not to memorize my lecture, but to try to interpret fairy tales themselves, for that is the only way to learn. Interpretation is an art, a craft actually, which finally depends on you yourself. The class where everyone interprets the same fairy tale is almost a confession. That cannot be avoided. And it's right, for you have to put your whole being into it.

We must begin by asking why in Jungian psychology we are interested in myths and fairy tales. Dr. Jung once said that it is in fairy tales that one can best study the comparative anatomy of the psyche. In myths or legends, or any other more elaborate mythological material, we get at the basic patterns of the human psyche through a lot of the cultural material. But in fairy tales there is much less specific cultural-conscious material, and therefore they mirror the basic patterns of the psyche more clearly.

One of the things that other psychological schools throw at our heads is that we analysts see archetypes everywhere, that our patients apparently dream about archetypes every night, but their patients never produce such material. If the analyst does not know what archetypal motifs are, naturally he does not notice them; he interprets them personally by linking them up with personal memories. In order to be able to spot archetypal material, we have first to have a general knowledge of it—one important reason why we try to learn as much as possible about these motifs and their different setups.

But there is another reason that has proved even more important practically and leads to more essential problems. If someone has a dream and you already have the anamnesis—that is, his general outer and inner life story—even if you try to refrain from doing so, you usually have made a kind of general hypothesis about what the dreamer's problem is: that this is a mother-bound man or a father-bound daughter, an animus-ridden woman, or God knows what else. Suppose, for instance, you have the hypothesis that a certain analysand is greatly bothered by her animus, and when she brings you the dream of a burglar, which frightened her terribly, then you have an "Aha! There we have it!" reaction. You don't notice that you have not interpreted the dream but have only recognized in it what you guessed. You linked it up with what you already intuitively supposed to be the trouble. Then you call the burglar an animus figure, and it looks like an objective interpretation. But you have not really learned to interpret the dream scientifically, having *no* hypothesis as to what will emerge from its motifs. We should look at dreams as objectively as possible and then only at the end deduce a conclusion. For the dream gives a *new* message which neither the analyst nor the analysand knew before.

This objective method can best be learned by practicing with fairy tale motifs in which there is no personal setup and you have no personal knowledge of the conscious situation to help you.

Let us first consider: how does a fairy tale originate? If we are realistic we have to say that it originates at one particular moment; at a certain time a certain fairy tale must have come into being. How could that happen?

Max Lüthi shows that in legends and in local sagas, the hero of the story is a very human being.[13] A local saga is the sort of story which runs this way: "Do you see the beautiful castle up there? Well, you know, a story is told about it. There was once a shepherd who on a hot midsummer day tended his sheep around this castle and was suddenly seized by curiosity and thought he might go inside, though he had heard that there were ghosts there. So with trembling hands he opened the door and saw a white snake, which spoke to him in human speech and said that the shepherd should come with it, and if he would suffer three nights he could redeem it . . . ," or something like that. That is what is called a local saga. Now Lüthi showed, with a great many examples, that in those local sagas the hero is a human being whose feelings and reactions are told. For instance, it is said that the shepherd's heart beat violently when he opened the castle door, and he shivered when he was given the cold kiss of the snake, but he was courageous and stood it all. The story is told as though an ordinary human being were having a supernatural or parapsychological experience. But if you take a classical fairy tale, such as the Grimms' "Golden Bird," there the hero has no such feelings. If a lion comes toward him, he takes his sword and kills it. Nothing is said about his being frightened and shivering and then putting his sword down the lion's throat and scratching his head and asking himself what he had done. Because he is a hero, he just naturally kills the lion. So Lüthi says that the hero in a fairy tale is an *abstract figure* and not at all human. He is either completely black or completely white, with stereotyped reactions: he redeems the lady and kills the lion and is not afraid of the old woman in the woods. He is completely schematic.

After reading that I came across a story from a nineteenth-century family chronicle published in a Swiss paper on folklore.[14] The family still lives in Chur, the capital of Graubünden. The great-grandfather of the people who are still living had had a mill in some lonely village in the Alps, and one evening he had gone out to shoot a fox. When he took aim, the animal lifted its paw and said, "Don't shoot me!" and then disappeared. The miller went home rather shaken, because speaking foxes were not part of his everyday experience. There he found the mill water racing autonomously around the wheel. He shouted, asking who had put the mill into motion. Nobody had done it. Two days later he died. In spiritualistic or parapsychological records this is a typical story. All over the world such things sometimes happen before someone dies: instruments behave as if alive, clocks stop as if they were part of the dying owner, and various queer things occur.

Now a man who read this story in the chronicles of this family went presently to the village and asked the people there about the mill. The mill itself was in ruins. A few people said, "Yes, there was a mill up there and there was something uncanny about it. There was a spook there." So one sees how the story had degenerated. They all knew that it had something to do with death and a parapsychological event, but they did not remember anything special. There the Finnish school seems to be right in saying that in the retelling things get poorer, but then this same investigator found other old people who said, "Oh, yes, we remember the story. The miller went out to shoot the fox, and the fox said, 'Miller, don't shoot me. You remember how I ground the corn at Aunt Jette's.' And then at the funeral party a wineglass was broken, and Aunt Jette, the miller's aunt, went quite white, and everybody knew that she was the fox and that it was she who had killed the miller."

There is a general belief in witches taking the form of foxes. Witches are said to go out at night as fox souls, do much mischief in this form, and then return to their bodies, which have lain as if dead on their beds meanwhile. That can be "proved" because sometimes a hunter comes across a fox, shoots him and wounds him in the paw, and then in the morning Mrs. So-and-So is seen sneaking about with her arm in a sling, and when she is asked what has happened she won't say. Naturally she was the ghost-fox going around making mischief. There is a general archetypal belief which you come across in the Alps and in Austria as well as in Japan and China that witches and hysterical women have fox souls. So a general archetypal motif has been associated with our special fox story, and the story has been nicely enriched and made more coherent. It was as if the people had said that it was not satisfactory—why did the fox talk to the miller just before he died? So it was enriched with a witch story and projected onto the miller's aunt, who gave herself away at the funeral party. Another old woman in the village told the same story but added still another motif—that when the miller came home and saw the mill wheel turning, there was a fox running around on it.

That proved to me that Antti Aarne was wrong in thinking that stories always degenerate, for they can just as well improve and by self-amplification become enriched by the addition of archetypal motifs. If there is any fantasy and storytelling talent, they can become beautiful. My hypothesis is that probably the more original forms of folktales are local sagas and parapsychological stories, miraculous stories which are due to invasions from the collective unconscious in the form of waking hallucinations. Such things still happen; Swiss peasants experience them constantly, and they are the basis of folklore beliefs. When something strange happens, it gets gossiped about and handed on, just as rumors are handed on; then under favorable conditions the account gets enriched with already existing archetypal representations and slowly becomes a story.

It is interesting that in this story only one person now remembered the miller's personal name. In the other versions it was already "a miller." So as long as it is Miller So-and-So, it is still a local saga, but when it comes to "A miller once went to shoot a fox . . . ," then it begins to be a fairy tale, a general story in a form in which it could migrate to another village, for it is no longer bound to a particular mill and a particular man. So probably Lüthi's statement is correct: fairy tales are an abstraction. They are an abstraction from a local saga, condensed and made into a crystallized form, and thus they can be handed on and are better remembered because they appeal to the people.

Since I came across this idea that parapsychological experiences are at the bottom of the local sagas, this has been also discovered and presented by J. Wyrsch, "Sagen und ihre seelischen Hintergründe" (*Innerschweiz. Jahrb. für Heimatkunde,* Lucerne, 1943, Bd. 7), H. Burkhardt, "Psychologie der Erlebnissage," (dissertation, Zurich, 1951). The readers will find more on this in G. Isler's excellent thesis, "Die Sennenpuppe" (dissertation, Zurich, 1970).

LITERATURE REVIEW

Even before Claude Lévy-Strauss founded the school of structuralism, a meritorious Russian researcher, Vladimir Propp, in *Morphology of the Folktale* (Bloomington, Ind., 1958), tried to determine certain structures within fairy tales. He was then accepted by the school of structuralists as being one of their own. As it has been proved that Lévy-Strauss quoted from Jung without making reference to the fact,[15] his work can be ignored here. On the other hand, Gilbert Durand in "Les structures anthropologiques de l'imaginaire" (1960) made an essentially new contribution to structuralism.

It is not my intention to discuss here the many current sociological and feminist theories of fairy tales for, out of ideological prejudice or resentments, they distort the basic facts.

Concerning historical fairy tale reasearch, Felix Karlinger's

Grundzüge einer Geschichte des Märchens im deutschen Sprachraum (Darmstadt: Wiss. Buchges., 1983) should be mentioned, as well as the collected volumes *Wege der Märchenforschung* (Darmstadt: Wiss. Buchges., 1973), of which Karlinger is the editor.

In my opinion, important non-Jungian contributions to comparative research in mythology have been made by Franz von Essen (in the *Symbolon* volumes, which at the time were published by Julius Schwabe) and Heino Gehrts in *Des Märchen und das Opfer: Untersuchungen zum europäischen Brüdermärchen* (Kassel, 1980). For both authors, see also *Vom Menschenbild im Märchen* (Kassel, 1980).

Thus we arrive at essential literature in depth psychology. In the form of an unrevised reprint there exists Herbert Silberer's work of 1914, *Probleme der Mystik und ihrer Symbolik* (Darmstadt: Wiss. Buchges., 1961), which also contains texts on dream and fairy tale interpretation from a psychoanalytical standpoint. Later works written from a Freudian point of view are Ottokar Wittgenstein's *Märchen, Träume, Schicksale* (Fischer Taschenbuch, 1981) and Bruno Bettelheim's *Uses of Enchantment: The Meaning and Importance of Fairy Tales* (London: Thames and Hudson, 1976). There is additional material by Wilhelm Laiblin published in the collected volume *Märchenforschung und Tiefenpsychologie* (Darmstadt: Wiss. Buchges., 1975).

And now to Jungian literature. Jung's own theories are to be found mainly in his early work *Symbols of Transformation* and in his later work with Karl Kerényi, *Science of Mythology* (London: Ark Paperbacks 1985). Jung wrote specifically about fairy tales in "The Phenomenology of the Spirit in Fairytales" (cw 9i, chap. 5). But clearly one can find interpretations of archetypal motifs throughout all his work. For a general introduction, I recommend Hedwig von Beits three-volume work *Symbolik des Märchens* (cf. also Max Lüthi's discussion in vol. 2: Gegensatz und Erneuerung, in *Neue Zürcher Zeitung,* no. 2806/07 (1957), as well as the work of Wilhelm

Laiblin, op. cit. and "Der goldene Vogel: Zur Symbolik der Individuation im Volksmärchen," in *Jugend gestern und heute* (Stuttgart: Klett, 1961), and *Wachstum und Wandlung: Zur Phänomenologie und Symbolik menschlicher Reifung* (Darmstadt: Wiss. Buchges., 1974); Hans Dieckmann, *Gelebte Märchen: Praxis der analytischen Psychologie* (Hildesheim 1983), as well as *Märchen und Symbole: Tiefenpsychologische Deutung orientalischer Märchen* (Fellbach: Bonz, 1984); but also Erich Neumann's interpretation of the Apuleius fairy tale, *Amor and Psyche: The Psychic Development of the Feminine* (Princeton, N.J.: Princeton University Press, 1971); Emma Jung, "Die Anima als Naturwesen," in *Studien zur analytischen Psychologie C. G. Jungs,* vol. 2 (Zürich: Rascher, 1955); Aniela Jaffé, "Bilder und Symbole aus E. T. A. Hoffmanns Märchen 'Der Goldene Topf,' " in C. G. Jung, *Gestaltungen aus dem Unbewussten* (Zurich, 1950); Sibylle Birkhäuser-Oeri, "Die Mutter im Märchen" (Fellbach: Bonz 1983); Marie-Louise von Franz, "Bei der schwarzen Frau: Deutungsversuch eines Märchens," in *Studien zur analytischen Psychologie C. G. Jungs,* vol. 2 (Zurich: Rascher, 1955), pp. 1–41, *The Feminine in Fairy Tales,* rev. ed. (Boston & London: Shambhala Publications, 1993), *Shadow and Evil in Fairy Tales,* rev. ed. (Boston & London: Shambhala Publications, 1995), *Individuation in Fairy Tales,* rev. ed. (Boston and London: Shambhala Publications, 1990), and *The Psychological Meaning of Redemption Motifs in Fairy Tales* (Toronto, 1980).

I am skipping popular literature here.

Thus we arrive at the sources which are important for the purpose of amplification. Of the earlier material, the ten-volume *Handwörterbuch des deutschen Aberglaubens,* which was brought into existence by von Bächtold-Stäubli, edited by Hoffmann-Krayer (Berlin, 1927–1942), must be recommended, as well as the basic work of Johannes Bolte and Georg Polivka, *Anmerkungen zu den Kinder- und Hausmärchen der Brüder Grimm,* 5 vols. (Leipzig 1913–1932), and the *Handwörterbuch des deutschen Märchens* (Berlin,

1930–1940), edited by Lutz Mackensen. As a new parallel work, one can recommend the *Enzyklopädie des Märchens: Handwörterbuch zur historischen und vergleichenden Erzählforschung* (Berlin, 1977ff.), which has filled four and a half volumes to the present time.

It is not my general practice to recommend symbol dictionaries, which for the most part are superficial and irritating. An exception to this, however, is in my opinion the recommendable four-volume *Dictionaire des symboles* (Paris: Laffont, 1969/Seghers, 1973), which contains excellent contributions to otherwise little-known African mythology.

Of interest among the works important for research into symbolism would primarily be the comprehensive work of Manfred Lurker, *Bibliographie zur Symbolkunde* (Baden-Baden: Heintz, 1964; Bibliotheca Bibliographica Aurelliana XII). In addition, I recommend R. B. Onian's *The Origin of European Thought* (Cambridge, 1952ff.), in which we can find very interesting material about body parts and body functions. Worth reading on individual themes are Arnold van Gennep, *Les rites de passage* (Paris, 1909), as well as Otto Huth, "Das Sonnen- Mond- und Sternenkleid" (manuscript) and "Der Glasberg des Volksmärchens," in *Symbolon 2*, 1955). Concerning the mythology of antiquity, I recommend the work of Karl Kerényi, above all *The Gods of the Greeks* and *The Heroes of the Greeks* (Thames and Hudson, 1979), and Mircea Eliade's work, above all *Myths, Dreams and Mysteries* (London: Harvill Press, 1907), *Shamanism: Archaic Techniques of Ecstasy* (New York: Bollingen Foundation, 1964), *The Forge and the Crucible* (University of Chicago Press, 1978) and *Cosmos and History: The Myth of the Eternal Return* (New York: Harper, 1959), as well as Joseph Campbell, *The Hero with a Thousand Faces* (Princeton, N.J.: Princeton University Press, 1968), and *Marks of the Gods*, 4 vols. (Penguin Books, 1981).

Current orientation concerning newly published literature can be found in the *Journal of Folklore Fellows Communication* (Helsinki/London) and in *Fabula* (Berlin).

2

FAIRY TALES, MYTHS, AND OTHER ARCHETYPAL STORIES

Personally, I think it likely that the most frequent way in which archetypal stories originate is through individual experiences of an invasion by some unconscious content, either in a dream or in a waking hallucination—some event or some mass hallucination whereby an archetypal content breaks into an individual life. That is always a numinous experience. In primitive societies practically no secret is ever really kept, so this numinous experience is always talked about and becomes amplified by any other existing folklore which will fit in. Thus it develops, just as rumors do.

Such invasions of the collective unconscious into the field of experience of a single individual probably, from time to time, create new nuclei of stories and also keep alive the already existing material. For instance, such a story will locally reinforce the belief in fox-witches. The belief existed before, but this story will keep alive or modernize or bring a new version of the old idea that witches in the form of foxes go about killing or bewitching people. These psychological events, which always reach an individual first, are to my mind the source and factor which keep the motifs in folklore alive.

It has been suggested that people know certain fairy tale motifs and stories and then pin them onto a local situation. Let us say that there is a girl in a village who commits suicide by jumping off the cliffs. Ten years later this suicide due to an unhappy love affair might be surrounded by a classical fairy-tale suicide motif. I think that this could easily happen, but I have not yet found any striking example where one could prove every step. Probably we have to reckon with *two* ways and can say that when a story is rooted somewhere, it becomes a local saga; and when it is cut off and wanders about, like a water plant cut off from its roots and carried away, then it becomes more of an abstract fairy tale, which, when it once more takes root, becomes more of a local saga. One could use the simile of a corpse, the fairy tale being the bones or the skeleton, the part which is not destroyed, for it is the most basic and eternal nucleus of the whole thing. It most simply shows the archetypal basic structure.

The same problem about the difference between a local story and a fairy tale has arisen in other ways and with much controversy about the relationship of myth and fairy tale. E. Schwyzer, a classical scholar, has, for instance, shown that the Hercules myth is built up out of single scenes, all of which are fairy tale motifs. He showed that this myth must have been a fairy tale which had been enriched and lifted to the literary level of a myth. Just as wisely fighting for the opposite theory, some people contend that fairy tales are degenerated myths. They believe that originally populations had only myths and that if the social and religious order of a population decayed, then the remains of that myth survived in the form of fairy tales.

There is a certain amount of truth in this theory of the "decayed myth." For example, in *Die Märchen der Weltliteratur (The Fairy Tales of World Literature),*[16] one finds in the volume of Greek fairy tales slightly distorted episodes of the *Odyssey:* a prince sails to an island where there is a big fish or ogre, and he blinds that one-eyed ogre and hides under the belly of a big ram and creeps out of the monster's cave. That was how Ulysses escaped from the Cyclops's cave, so that story has been preserved till today. I do not, therefore, think it far-fetched to say that this tale is a remnant of the Ulysses story. It has survived and has nowadays become an ordinary Greek folktale. The story has convinced me that big myths can decay with the civilization to which they belonged and the basic motifs can survive as fairy tale motifs and migrate or stay in the same country. As with the local saga, I think we have to reckon with both possibilities. To me the fairy tale is like the sea, and the sagas and myths are like the waves upon it; a tale rises to be a myth and sinks down again into being a fairy tale. Here again we come to the same conclusion: fairy tales mirror the more simple but also more basic structure—the bare skeleton—of the psyche.

The myth is something national. If you think of the Gilgamesh myth, you think of the Sumerian-Hittite-Babylonian civilization, for Gilgamesh belongs there and cannot be put into Greece or Rome, just as the Hercules and Ulysses myths belong to Greece and cannot be imagined in a Maori setup. If one studies the psychological implications of myths, one sees that they very much express the national character of the civilization in which they originated and have been kept alive. They have a beautiful form because generally either priests or poets, and sometimes priest-poets—in certain civilizations that is the same thing—have endeavored to give them a solemn, ceremonious, and poetical form. With this form we have in the myth a conscious cultural addition, which makes its interpretation easier in some ways, for certain things are said more explicitly. Gilgamesh, for instance, is said to be favored by Shamash, the sun god, about whom material can be collected and tied up into the amplification, providing all that is necessary. Sometimes a fairy tale hero also has solar qualities, but these may be indicated only by a small detail—for instance, that he has golden hair. There is no mention of his being favored by a specific sun god.

So it can be said that the basic structure or archetypal elements of a myth are built into a formal expression, which links it up with the cultural collective consciousness of the nation in which it originated, and that therefore, in a way, it is closer to consciousness and to known historical material. In some ways it is easier to interpret, being less fragmentary. Often it is also much more beautiful and impressive in form than the fairy tale, so that some scholars are seduced into saying that the myth is the big thing and the rest just miserable remnants. On the other hand, by lifting such an archetypal motif to a cultural and national level and by linking it with religious traditions and poetic forms, it more specifically expresses the problems of that nation in that cultural period, but *loses* some of its generally human character. Ulysses, for example, is the essence of the Hermetic-Mercurial Greek intellect and can easily be compared to trickster heroes of other nations. But the Ulysses myth as a whole is more specific and Greek. It can be said to have lost certain general human features.

For us the study of fairy tales is very important because they depict the *general human* basis. They are especially important if one analyzes people from the other end of the world; if a Hindu or an Australian walks into the consulting room of a European analyst who has only studied his own myth, he will not find a human bridge to the analysand. If, however, the analyst has the knowledge of those basic human structures, he will be able to contact him. I have read of a missionary in the South Sea Islands who says that the simplest way to contact those people is by telling them fairy tales. It is a language in which each understand the other. If he told some big myth, that would not work so well. He has to use the basic material in its simple form because that is the expression of the most general and, at the same time, basic human structure. Because the fairy tale is beyond cultural and racial differences, it can migrate so easily. Fairy tale language seems to be the international language of all mankind—of all ages and of all races and cultures.

Sometimes when I do not understand a fairy tale, I use myths as parallels because the greater closeness to consciousness of the myth material often gives me an idea about the meaning. So do not leave out myths, because they can be used to make a bridge when you do not see what the fairy tale material means; sometimes the tale is so terribly remote from one's own collective-conscious world.

With religious myths we still have to make a subdivision because some are told in connection with a ritual and others not. On a certain day the myth is told at a certain festival, and the song which belongs to a certain mythological event is sung. Or, in some schools—the Talmud school, for instance—there are the holy texts which are read on certain occasions and so are built into a liturgy of some kind. Then there are religious myths which are not built into a liturgy, the Gilgamesh epic, for example. That was generally retold at the king's court, but we do not know that it was ever built into a liturgy. Now those religious myths which are not built into a liturgy or not told at a certain ritual, or which do not comprise sacred knowledge, given either orally or in writing on certain occasions, I would classify with the myths I mentioned earlier.

But then we come to the specific case where, as liturgies or songs sung by certain priests, myths are built into religious rituals. In my opinion, such liturgical myths are not basically different from the others except that they have become a part of the conscious tradition of the nation; they have been integrated into the body of conscious knowledge of that nation, into its officially recognized body. That does not make them in any way secondary; it is only that they have been elaborated for a long time. Generally such myths have been influenced by historical traditions; these sacred texts and songs are very often almost unintelligible: they have been so worked upon that they merely allude to something that everybody knows. For example, we have some Christmas carols out of which, if you were to dig them up two thousand years from now and knew nothing about Christianity, you would not be able to make head nor tail. A German Christmas carol says, "Es ist ein Ros' entsprungen aus einer Wurzel zart" ("From a tender root a rose has blossomed forth"), and then there follow a few more remote allusions to an untouched virgin. Now assuming that you knew nothing about Christianity and discovered this carol, you would say that here is something about a rose and something about a virgin, but what does that mean? To us the song is intelligible because it alludes to a mystery we all know. With us the Christian teaching is so integrated that the many songs which refer to it are mere allusions; however, only archetypal motifs which have been meaningful to many people for many hundreds of years are treated in this fashion. If Christianity had been confined to a local sect in Asia Minor, it would have died with its myth and would not have attracted other material and would not have been elaborated. Extensive elaboration of the original material probably depends on the impact that the nuclear archetypal event has on people.

It has been suggested that perhaps Christianity could also have had its origins in a local saga and so have developed into a more general myth. In his book *Aion* Jung elaborates that the unknown and mysterious and impressive personality of Jesus of Nazareth, about whom we know very, very little, attracted an enormous number of projections, as, for instance, the symbols of the fish, the lamb, and many other archetypal symbols of the Self well known to humanity in general. Many of these, however, are not mentioned in the Bible—for example, the peacock, an early Christian symbol of the resurrection and of Christ. The whole web of existing mythological ideas of late antiquity had slowly crystallized around the personality of Christ. The specific features of Jesus of Nazareth are blurred to such an extent that we are mostly confronted by the symbol of the God-Man, which is amplified by many other archetypal symbols.

In this way the figure of Jesus is generalized, but in another way it is made specific, as can be seen in the fight of the early Church Fathers against the tendency of that time to say that Jesus Christ was just another Dionysus or another Osiris. People then were saying, "Oh, your Jesus Christ, we know him: we worship him in the form of Osiris." But then the Apologists were furious, saying that Jesus Christ was *not* the same; he was a new message. There then ensued that fight over the new message—that it was to be seen in another light and—such people said—must not be pulled regressively into those older myths. About Jesus people said, "But this is Osiris! This is our Dionysus! We have known the suffering and dismembered god from long ago." And they were half right: what they saw was the same general archetypal pattern. But the others were right too when they insisted that this was now a new cultural consciousness in a specific new form.

The same kind of thing happened when in South America the Conquistadores discovered the ritual of crucifixion among the aborigenes. Some Jesuit Father even said that the devil must have put it into those people's heads to weaken the possibility of their conversion. But the hypothesis of the archetypal disposition of the human psyche simplifies many of these questions, so that one does not need to get lost in unnecessary quarrels about the religious myths. The different versions are the different elaborations of various forms of the archetype. One could say that whenever an archetypal content of vital importance is constellated, it tends to become the central symbol of a new religion. When, however, an archetypal content belongs merely to the body of general human welfare and is not specifically constellated, it is handed on in the form of folklore. But at the time of Christ the idea of the God-Man—which had existed for ages—had become the eminently important message, the one thing that had now to be realized at all costs. That is why it became the new message, the new light. And its emotional impact has created all that we now call the Christian civilization (just as Buddha's enlightenment created all that we now call the Buddhist religion).

There is another problem connected with this. In his book *Primitive Culture,* Tylor tried, with this theory of animism, to derive fairy tales from ritual, claiming that not only should they be regarded as the remains of a decayed faith but that they are specifically the remains of an old ritual: the ritual died, but its story has survived in fairy tale form.[17] I do not believe this, because I think that the *basis* is not a ritual but an archetypal experience. However, rituals are so age-old that one can only guess how they may have originated. The best examples of how a ritual might have originated that I have found are in the following two stories.

One story is the autobiography of Black Elk, a medicine man belonging to the American Indian tribe of the Oglala Sioux.[18] As a boy, when Black Elk was suffering from a severe illness and was almost in a coma, he had a tremendous vision or revelation in which he was transported to the skies where many horses came to him from the four points of the compass, where then he met the Grandfather Spirits and was given the healing plant for his people. Deeply shaken by his vision, the youth kept it to himself, as any normal human being would do, but later on he developed an acute phobia about thunderstorms, so that when even a little cloud appeared on the horizon, he would shake with fear. This forced him to consult a medicine man, who told him that he was ill because he had kept his vision to himself and had not shared it with his tribe. The medicine man said to Black Elk, "Nephew, I know now what the trouble is! You must do what the bay horse in your vision wanted you to do. You must perform this vision for your people upon earth. You must have the horse-dance first for the people to see. Then the fear will leave you; but if you do not do this, something very bad will happen to you." So Black Elk, who was then seventeen, and his father and mother and some other members of the tribe gathered together the exact number of horses—a certain number of white, a certain number of black, a certain number of sorrel, a certain number of buckskin, and one bay horse for Black Elk to ride. Black Elk taught the songs that he had heard during his experience, and when the vision was enacted, it had a profound effect on the entire tribe, even a healing effect, with the result that the blind could see, the paralyzed walked, and other psychogenic diseases were cured. The tribe decided to perform it again, and I feel sure that it would have continued as a ritual if soon afterward the tribe had not been almost destroyed by the whites. In this account we are close to witnessing the way in which a ritual can originate.

I have found another trace of the origin of a ritual in an Eskimo tale reported by Knud Rasmussen.[19] Certain circumpolar Arctic tribes have an Eagle Festival. They send messengers out, with feathers glued onto their sticks, to invite the other tribes to a big feast. The hosts build a large igloo, sometimes a big wooden assembly house. Once a year the people come in their dog sledges. In the hall there is a stuffed eagle, and they dance, tell stories, exchange wives, and trade. The Eagle Festival is the big half-religious, half-profane meeting of all the tribes.

The story about the origin of the festival is that a lonely hunter once shot an especially beautiful eagle. He took it home, apparently with a rather guilty feeling, stuffed it, and kept it, and even felt impelled from time to time to give it a little food-sacrifice. Then once he was out on his skis, hunting, and got into a blizzard. He sat down and saw suddenly in front of him two men with sticks onto which feathers were glued. The men wore animal masks and ordered him to come along with them and to hurry. So in the blizzard he pulled himself up, and they went very fast, he with them and in great exhaustion. Then through the mist he saw a village from which came an uncanny booming noise. He asked what the drum was saying, and one of the men said very sadly, "A mother's heart is beating." They took him into the village and led him to a very dignified woman in black, and he suddenly realized that she was the eagle-mother of the eagle he had shot. The dignified eagle-mother said that he had treated her son very well and had paid him honor and she wished this to continue; that therefore she was now showing him her people (all the people were really eagles who had temporarily assumed human form), who would now show him the Eagle Festival; that he must try to memorize everything and then return to his tribe and report it to them and say she wanted this done every year. After the human eagles had performed the Eagle Festival, suddenly everything disappeared and the hunter found himself back in the snowstorm, numb and half-frozen. He dragged himself back to his village, assembled the men, and delivered the message, and from then on, they say, the Eagle Festival has been performed in this exactly prescribed way. The hunter, nearly frozen, had obviously fallen into a coma and, in this state of deep unconsciousness, had what we would call an archetypal vision. That is why everything disappeared suddenly and he found himself numb in the snow; that was the moment when he returned to consciousness and saw animal tracks in the snow beside him—the last vestiges of the "messengers."

There again you see how a ritual came into existence in a way parallel to that of Black Elk—namely, from the archetypal experience of an individual; and if the impact is strong enough, there is a need to spread it abroad and not keep it to oneself. I have met, on a small scale, similar things in analysis when an analysand had an archetypal experience and, naturally kept it to him or herself.

This is the natural reaction because it is one's personal secret and one does not want others to disparage it. But then other dreams came which said that the individual should stand up for this inner vision, tell it to the wife or the husband, saying, "I have had that experience and have to stick to it. That is why I now have to tell you about it, for otherwise you will not understand my behavior. I have to be loyal to the vision and act in accordance with it." In a close relationship one cannot suddenly begin to behave quite differently without any explanation. Or perhaps it must be communicated more widely, sometimes even to a group, as happened to Black Elk, to whom the medicine man said that his neurotic symptoms showed that Black Elk's vision was something which belonged to the tribe and was not his private secret.

From those two stories I concluded that this is a likely explanation of how a ritual can come into existence. In this Eskimoan example they say so themselves. We see again that the basis is an invasion of the archetypal world into the collective tribal consciousness of a group through the intermediary of an individual. One person experiences it first and then announces it to the others. Besides, if we really think about it, how else could it happen? It is the most obvious way for a ritual to have originated.

Minor invasions of the unconscious and dreams can still alter a ritual later. There is a famous thirty-year-old ritual among Australian primitives called Kunapipi, and a meritorious ethnologist, Berndt, has collected the dreams referring to it. The aborigines say that they dream about the ritual, and in his book *Kunapipi* Berndt gives a collection of their dreams, all of which had made some slight alteration or additions to the ritual.[20] The dream is told the tribe, and if the alteration is good and fitting, it is added to the ritual. In analyzing Catholics I have often seen that this still works in some way. Someone will dream about the Mass, and the dreamer's unconscious makes all sorts of propositions as to how something more could be added. I remember a nun who dreamed about the Mass, and the whole service was normal until the moment for the Sanctus came, but when the bell was rung, there was an interruption. In this most holy moment of the Mass, the moment of transformation, the bishop went into the pulpit and gave a short, prosaic, and down-to-earth exposition of what it meant that God became man, after which the Mass was resumed, as if that nun's unconscious desired to point out that some understanding of the mystery had been lost sight of.

There is still another type of archetypal story which might be worth mentioning. If you read *Fairy Tales of World Literature,* you will see that in certain ethnological setups what are called fairy tales are practically all animal tales, and even in the Grimm collection there are very many animal tales. According to Laurens van der Post's *The Heart of the Hunter,* about eighty percent of the Bushman tales are animal tales.[21] The word *animal* is not very good in this connection because although the characters are animals, everyone knows that these animals are at the same time anthropomorphic beings. Just as in the Eagle Festival story, in which there are eagles who are human beings and two minutes later are again eagles, there is the same idea in Bushman stories; sometimes they even say, "The hyena, which naturally was a human being, said to his wife . . . " Very often, however, this is not said explicitly, but in the story the hyena takes a bow, or makes a boat, and so on. These figures are human beings in the shape of animals, or animals in the form of human beings; they are not what we nowadays would call animals.

Anthropologists quarrel about whether they are animals disguised as human beings or human beings disguised as animals. But that is idiotic, to my mind. They are just what they are! They are animals *and* human beings. No primitive would puzzle about it; there is no contradiction. From our standpoint they are symbolic animals, for we make another distinction: we say the animal is the carrier of the projection of human psychic factors. As long as there is still an archaic identity, and as long as you have not taken the projection back, the animal and what you project onto it are identical; they are one and the same thing. You see it beautifully in those animal stories which represent archetypal human tendencies. They are human because they really do not represent animal instincts but *our* animal instincts, and in that sense they are really anthropomorphic. Let us say, for instance, that the tiger in a story represents greed; it is not the real tiger's greed that is represented, but *our own tigerish greed*. It is when we are as greedy as tigers that we dream about a tiger. So it is an anthropomorphic tiger. Such animal stories are exceedingly frequent, and there are many investigators who assert that they are the most ancient type of mythological story. I am very much tempted to believe that one of the most ancient and basic forms of archetypal tales have this form—stories about anthropoid animal beings, where fox speaks to mouse and hare talks to cat.

Because I am known as being interested in fairy tales, I have again and again been pulled in by families to tell their children fairy tales, and I have seen that below a certain age children prefer animal stories. When you start stories about princes and princesses being stolen by the devil, then they ask, "What is the devil?" and so on. They need too many explanations. But if you say, "The dog said to the cat . . . ," then they listen most eagerly. So it seems to be the basic material, the deepest and most ancient form of tale.

3

A METHOD OF PSYCHOLOGICAL
INTERPRETATION

The next problem is the method of interpretation of fairy tales. How do we approach the meaning of a fairy tale?—or stalk it, rather, because it is really like stalking a very evasive stag. And why do we interpret? Again and again investigators and specialists on mythology attack Jungians on the grounds that a myth speaks for itself; that you have only to unravel what it says, and you do not need psychological interpretation; that the psychological interpretation is only reading something into it which is not in it; and that the myth with all its details and amplifications is quite clear in itself. This seems to me to be half true. It is in the same way true, as Jung says, that the dream is its own best explanation. That means the interpretation of the dream is never as good as the dream itself. The dream is the best possible expression of inner facts, and you could just as well say that the fairy tale and the myth are the best possible expressions. So, in that sense, those who hate interpretation and say the myth is enough are right. The interpretation is a darkening of the original light which shines in the myth itself. But if someone tells you a marvelous dream and is very excited and you sit back and say, "Yes, there you had that dream," he will say, "But I want to know what it means!" You may then answer, "Well, look at the dream! It tells you all it can. It is its own best possible interpretation." That has its merits because then the dreamer may go home and keep turning the dream around in his mind and suddenly get his own illumination about it. And that process of rubbing one's churinga stone—treating the dream as one might a churinga stone or a talisman till it gives you some strength—is not interrupted by a third person who interposes himself.

On the other hand, this method is often not sufficient, for the most amazing and beautiful dream messages do not get over. Then the dreamer is like somebody who has an enormous bank balance and does not know about it, or who has lost the safe key or deposit number. And what is the use of that? It is certainly true that one should be tactful, hoping and waiting to see whether the dream will not build its own bridge toward the dreamer's consciousness and whether that process cannot take place by itself, because it is certainly more genuine and people are much more impressed by what they find out about their dreams than if one presents them with even a good interpretation. But very often those millions in the bank are not made use of and people are impoverished. There is another reason why interpretation has still to be practiced: people tend to interpret their own dreams and myths within the framework of their conscious assumptions. For instance, a thinking type will naturally tend to extract only some kind of philosophical thought which he feels is contained in the dream, and he will, for instance, overlook the emotional message and the feeling circumstances. Then I have also known people, men especially, who, when they are caught in their own anima mood, project their mood into the dream and perhaps see only its negative aspects.

The interpreter is useful, for he says, "Yes, look here! The dream begins very badly, but the lysis is very good! Surely it says that you are still a fool or half-blind, but it also says there is a treasure." Interpretation gets a bit more objective. The dream or tale is not only pulled into the already existing trend of conscious-ness. Hence, we practice interpretation in analysis.

As I have already suggested, interpretation is an art or craft that can be learned only by practice and experience. However, there are some rules to guide one.

Just as for a dream, we divide the archetypal story into the four stages of the classic drama, beginning with the exposition (time and place). In fairy tales time and place are always evident because they begin with "once upon a time" or something similar, which means in timelessness and spacelessness—the realm of the collec-tive unconscious. For example some tales begin with:

"Far beyond the end of the world and even beyond the Seven Dog Mountains there was once a king . . . "

"At the end of the world, where the world comes to an end with a wall of boards . . . "

"In the time when God still walked about on earth . . . "

There are many poetical ways of expressing this once-upon-a-time, which, following Eliade, most mythologists now call the *illud tem-pus,* that timeless eternity, now and ever.

Then we turn to the *dramatis personae* (the people involved). I recommend counting the number of people at the beginning and end. If a fairy tale begins, "The king had three sons," one notices that there are four characters, but the mother is lacking. The story may end with one of the sons, his bride, his brother's bride, and another bride—that is, four characters again but in a different setup. Having seen that the mother is lacking at the beginning and there are three women at the end, one would suspect that the whole story is about redeeming the female principle, as in one of the stories I shall use later as an illustration.

Now we proceed to the naming of the problem. You will find this in the form of the old king who is sick, for instance, or the king who discovers every night that golden apples are stolen from his tree, or that his horse has no foal, or that his wife is ill and somebody says she needs the water of life. Some trouble always comes at the beginning of the story, because otherwise there would be no story. So you define the trouble psychologically as well as you can and try to understand what it is.

Then comes the *peripeteia*—the ups and downs of the story—which can be short or long. This can go on for pages because there can be many *peripeteiai;* or perhaps you have only one, and then you generally get to the climax, the decisive point, where either the whole thing develops into a tragedy or it comes out right. It is the height of the tension. Then, with very few exceptions, there is a lysis, or sometimes a catastrophe. One could also say a positive or negative lysis, an end result, which is either that the prince gets his princess and they marry and are happy ever after, or they all fall into the sea and disappear and are never heard of again (the latter being either positive or negative, depending on how one looks at it). Sometimes in very primitive stories, however, there is neither lysis nor catastrophe, but the story just peters out. It suddenly gets stupid and fades away, exactly as if the storyteller were suddenly to lose interest and fall asleep.

Then again, there may be a double end to the lysis, something you don't find in other kinds of legends or mythic materials: namely, a happy ending followed by a negative remark by the story-teller. For instance, "And they married and there was a big feast, and they had beer and wine and a marvelous piece of meat, and I went to the kitchen but when I wanted to take some, the cook gave me a kick in the pants, and I rushed here to tell you the story." Or the Russians sometimes end: "They married and were very happy. They drank a lot of beer and wine, but mine ran through my beard and I never swallowed any." Or some Gypsies say: "They married and were happy and rich to the end of their lives, but we poor devils are standing here shivering and sucking our teeth with hunger"—and then they go around with the hat, collecting.

These formulas at the end of a fairy tale are a *rite de sortie,* because a fairy tale takes you far away into the childhood dream world of the collective unconscious, where you may not stay. Now imagine that you live in a peasant house and you stay in the fairy tale mood, and then you have to go to the kitchen. If you have not kicked yourself out of the story, you will certainly burn the roast because you will continue to think about the prince and the princess. So the story must be accentuated at the end with "Yes, that is the fairy tale world, but here we are in bitter reality. We must return to our everyday work and may not be absent-minded and puzzle about the story." We have to be switched out of the fairy tale world.

So much for the general method by which we watch the structure and bring some order into our material; and, we should remember especially to count the characters, and to notice the number symbolism and the part that it plays. There is another way which I sometimes adopt, but which cannot be done with all stories. For instance, there is a Russian story, "The Virgin Czar," in which the czar has three sons. You could diagram it as shown in the illustration on page 42.

First there is a male quaternity in which the mother is lacking, and the hero, the fourth of the system, goes into the Beyond (into the unconscious, we would say), where there are three witches (Baba Yagas) and the Princess Mary, whom the hero wins. At the end Mary is redeemed by the hero, and they marry and two sons are born. So there is a quaternity which is purely male and one purely female, and in the end we have (in the middle) a mixed quaternity of three males and one female. You cannot make this kind of pattern with all stories, so do not try to ram it in when it

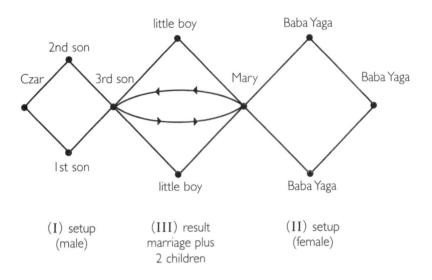

little boy   Baba Yaga

2nd son

Czar   3rd son   Mary   Baba Yaga

1st son

little boy   Baba Yaga

(I) setup   (III) result   (II) setup
(male)   marriage plus   (female)
          2 children

is not there. There are a lot of stories structured in this way, however, so look to see if there is such a pattern. If there is not, that is also revealing, because a lack of pattern tells you something too, as does an irregular pattern in science. The exception belongs also to the regular phenomenon, but then you have to explain why.

To continue the rules of our method: we simply take the first symbol. Let's say there was an old king who was sick because he needed the water of life, or there was a mother who had a disobedient daughter; and now we have to amplify this, which means that we must look up all the parallel motifs we can get hold of. I say *all* because initially you will probably not be able to find too many; when you get about two thousand you might stop! In the Russian tale "The Virgin Czar," for instance, the story begins with an old czar and his three sons. The youngest son is the Dummling hero of the story. I once compared the czar's behavior to that of the main function and the son's to that of the fourth function, but it was disputed. It cannot be proved from this tale because the czar is not eliminated at the end, nor does he fight his son. But if you draw in all other parallel stories, then it becomes quite clear that the czar represents the outworn main function and the third son is the bringer of renewal, that is, the inferior function.

Thus we have to look at the comparative material before we can say anything definite. We have to ask whether that motif occurs in other tales, and how it is in other tales, and take an average, and only then is our interpretation on a *relatively* secure basis. For example, there might be a fairy tale in which a white dove misbehaves. And you say that the white dove represents a witch or a wizard. Well, in *this* story it may be, but if you look up what a white dove usually means you will be astonished. As a rule, in the Christian tradition the white dove signifies the Holy Ghost, and in fairy tales it generally means a loving woman, a Venus-like woman. Therefore you have to ask why something which usually is a symbol for positive Eros appears to be negative in this particular story. You have a different slant on the image than if you had not taken the trouble to look up other stories. Suppose you were a doctor performing your first autopsy and found the appendix on the left and did not know, by comparative anatomy, that normally the appendix belongs on the right. It is the same with fairy tales: *you have to know the average setup,* and that is why you need comparative material—to know the comparative anatomy of all the symbols. That background will help you to understand the specific much better, and only then can you fully appreciate the exception. *Amplification means enlarging through collecting a quantity of parallels.* When you have a collection of parallels, then you pass on to the next motif and in this way go through the whole story.

There are two more steps to be taken, for next we have to construct the context. Let's say that in the fairy tale there is a mouse, and you have amplified it but see that this mouse behaves in a specific way. For instance, you have read that mice represent the souls of the dead, witches, that they are the bringers of the plague, and they are also soul-animals because when somebody dies, a mouse comes out of his corpse or he appears in the form of a mouse, and so on. You look at the mouse in your story, and some of the mice in your amplifications fit your mouse and explain it while others do not. Now what do you do? In such a case I first take the mice which explain my mouse, but I keep the other mice in my pocket, or in a footnote, because sometimes, later in the story, some of the other aspects of the mouse will appear in another constellation. Let's say that in your fairy tale it is a positive mouse and there is no witch-mouse around, but later in the story there *is* something about a witch. Then you say, "Aha! There is a connection between these two images, so it is a good thing that I know that mice are also witches."

Then comes the last essential step, which is the interpretation itself—the task of translating the amplified story into psychological language. There is a danger of remaining half within the mystical mode of expression and talking about "the terrible mother who is overcome by the hero." Such a statement becomes correct only if we say: "The inertia of unconsciousness is overcome by an impulse toward a higher level of consciousness." That is, we must use strictly psychological language. Only then do we know what the interpretation is.

Now if you are critical-minded you will say, "All right, but then you simply replace one myth by another—by our myth, the Jungian myth, you could call it." There one can only answer: "Yes, we do that, but consciously; we know that we are doing it, and we know quite well that if in two hundred years someone were to read our interpretations, they would say, 'Isn't that funny! They translated the fairy tale myth into Jungian psychology and thought that was it! But we know that it is . . . ' " And they will bring a new interpretation, and ours will be counted as one of the outgrown interpretations—an illustration of how such material was regarded at that time. We are aware of this possibility and know that our interpretations are relative, that they are not absolutely true. But we interpret for the same reason as that for which fairy tales and myths were told: because it has a vivifying effect and gives a satisfactory reaction and brings one into peace with one's unconscious instinctive substratum, just as the telling of fairy tales always did. Psychological interpretation is our way of telling stories; we still have the same need and we still crave the renewal that comes from understanding archetypal images. We know quite well that it is just our myth. We explain an *X* by a *Y* because *Y* seems to click for us now. One day this will no longer be the case, and there will be the need for a *Z* as an explanation. Therefore we should never present our interpretation with the undertone of "This is it." That would be cheating. We can only say in psychological language what the myth *seems* to represent and then modernize the myth in this psychological form. The criterion is: Is it satisfactory and does it click with me and with other people? And do my own dreams agree? When I make an interpretation, I always watch my dreams to see if they agree. If they do, then I know that the interpretation is as good as I can make it—that in relation to my own nature I have interpreted the material satisfactorily. If my psyche says, "That is all right," then I can stop, but if it says, "You have not answered *this* yet," then I know that I must go further. If my dreams make no further demands, there still may be other revelations in the story, but I have reached my own limits; I cannot go beyond myself. Then I can sit back satisfied, having eaten what I could digest. There is a lot more meat there, but I cannot digest it psychically.

4

A TALE INTERPRETED:
"THE THREE FEATHERS"

———— ❧❧❧❧❧❧ ————

We can now proceed to the more practical problems of interpretation. For didactic reasons I have taken for interpretation a very simple Grimms' fairy tale, not with the idea of making it fascinating or interesting, but simply to show you the method of interpretation. I will try to show you how to proceed and how you get at the meaning of such a story. It is called "The Three Feathers."[22]

There was once a king who had three sons. Two were intelligent, but the third did not talk much and was stupid and was called Dummling. The king was old and weak and thought about his death and did not know which of his sons should inherit the kingdom. So he told them to go out into the world, and the one who brought him the most beautiful carpet would be king when he died. To prevent any quarreling he went outside the castle, blew three feathers into the air, and said, "As they fly, so you must go." One feather went toward the east, the other to the west, and the third just a little way straight ahead, where it fell to the ground. So one brother went to the right, the other to the left, and they laughed at Dummling, who had to stay where the third feather had fallen.

Dummling sat down and was very sad, but then suddenly he noticed that there was a trapdoor beside the feather. He lifted it up, found steps descending, and went down into the earth. There he came to another door, at which he knocked, and from the inside he heard:

> *Virgin, green and small,*
> *Shrivel leg,*
> *Shrivel leg's dog,*
> *Shrivel back and forth.*
> *Let's see who is outside.*

The door opened and Dummling saw an enormous fat toad sitting there, surrounded by a circle of little toads. The fat toad asked him what he wanted, and he answered that he would like to have the finest and most beautiful carpet. The toad called a young toad, saying:

> *Virgin, green and small,*
> *Shrivel leg,*
> *Shrivel leg's dog,*
> *Shrivel back and forth.*
> *Bring me the big box.*

The young toad fetched the big box, which the big toad opened, and from it she gave Dummling a beautiful carpet, a carpet so beautiful and so delicate that it could never have been woven on earth. He thanked her for it and climbed up again.

The two other brothers thought their youngest brother too silly ever to be able to find anything, so they bought some coarse linen stuff which the first shepherd woman they met was wearing around her body and took it home to the king. At the same time Dummling came home with his beautiful carpet, and when the king saw it he said, "By rights the kingdom should go to the youngest." But the other two gave their father no peace, saying that it was impossible to give Dummling the kingdom because he was so stupid, and they asked for another competition.

So the king said that the one who could bring the most beautiful ring should have the kingdom. Again he performed the same ritual with the three feathers. Again the two eldest went to the east and to the west, and for Dummling the feather went straight ahead and fell down by the door in the ground. Again he went down to the fat toad and told her that he wanted the most beautiful ring. She again had the big box fetched and from it gave him a ring which gleamed with precious stones and was so beautiful that no goldsmith on earth could have made it. The other two again laughed about Dummling who wanted to hunt for a gold ring, and they went to no trouble but knocked the nails out of an old cartwheel and brought that to the king. When Dummling showed his gold ring, the king again said that the kingdom belonged to him. But the two elder brothers tormented the king until he set a third competition and said that the one who brought home the most beautiful wife should have the kingdom. He blew the three feathers again, and they fell as before.

Dummling went to the fat toad and said that he had to take home the most beautiful woman. "Oh," said the toad, "the most beautiful woman is not at hand just now, but you shall have her." She gave him a hollowed-out carrot to which six mice were harnessed, and Dummling said sadly, "What shall I do with that?" The toad answered that he should take one of her little toads and put it into the carriage. He took one at random out of the circle and put it in the yellow carriage. It had scarcely sat down before it was transformed into a beautiful girl, the carrot into a coach, and the six mice into six horses. He kissed the girl and drove away with the horses and brought her to the king. His brothers, who had not taken any trouble to look for a beautiful woman, came back with the first two peasant women they met. When the king saw them he said, "The kingdom goes to the youngest after my death." But the two brothers again deafened the king with their cries, saying that they couldn't permit that, and requested that the one whose wife could jump through a ring which hung in the middle of the room should have the preference. They thought that the peasant women would be able to do that because they would be strong but that the delicate girl would jump to her death. The old king agreed, and the two peasant women jumped through the ring, but they were so awkward that they fell and broke their thick arms and legs. Thereupon the beautiful girl whom Dummling had brought sprang as lightly as a deer through the ring. So no further objection was possible. Dummling got the crown and ruled in wisdom for a long time.

You will probably recognize in this simple classical story an accumulation of well-known motifs. Bolte and Polivka say that this fairy tale was found by the Grimms in 1819 in Zwehrn, Germany, and that there is also another German version, from the region of Hesse, which has slight variations.[23] I don't wish to repeat the whole story, but in this other version, instead of a carpet it is linen, and when Dummling goes down into the earth he does not find toads but a beautiful girl who is weaving linen, so there is not quite the same problem. She also gives him a carpet and only turns into a frog when she comes up to the surface of the earth, which means that under the ground she appears to him as a beautiful woman, but as soon as she comes to join him on the earth she turns into a frog. When the frog arrives at the king's court in the carriage, it cries out, "Kiss me and *versenk dich.*" *Versenken* really intimates meditation, so it would mean "sink down into yourself in meditation"—which seems a very strange expression for a frog in a fairy tale. It repeats this three times, so Dummling takes the frog and jumps into the water with it, for he has understood *versenken* as meaning that he should submerge himself in the water, which is also a meaning of the word. The moment he kisses it and jumps into the water, it turns back into a beautiful woman.

There are other Hessian variations where the three feathers are replaced by three apples which are rolled in different directions, and there is a French variation where the only change is that the toad is replaced by a white cat. I will not repeat all the possibilities but will mention a few of the more frequent ones. Often the motif of the feathers is replaced by arrows which the father shoots in three directions. And then the bride is either a toad, a frog, a white cat, an ape, a lizard, a puppet, a rat, a stocking, or a hopping nightcap—not even living objects—and sometimes a turtle.

At the end of all these variations—among which the Russian are the most interesting—there is a short annotation explaining that the motif of blowing a feather to indicate the direction the sons should take was a general medieval custom in many countries. If people did not know where to go, if they were lost at a cross-roads or had no special plan, they would take a feather, blow on it, and walk in whichever direction the wind took it. That was a very common kind of oracle by which you could be guided. There are many medieval stories referring to this and even folklore expressions such as "I shall go where the feather blows." In northern countries and in certain Russian and Italian versions, instead of feathers and arrows or rolling apples, there are spheres or balls.

We will begin with the first few sentences. Our exposition runs: There was a king who had three sons. Two were intelligent, the third stupid, and the old king did not know to whom he should give his kingdom. That shows the opening psychological situation. The last sentence sets the problem, which is who should have the kingdom.

The opening situation of the king and his three sons is exceedingly frequent. The Grimm collection alone, which is merely a fraction of all exciting possibilities, has at least fifty or sixty such stories that start off with the king and his three sons. That is not the normal family, for there is neither mother nor sister, and the initial setup of people is purely masculine. The female element, which you expect in a complete family, is not represented. The main action is concerned with the finding of the right female, upon which depends the inheritance of the kingdom. One further point is that the hero does not perform any masculine deeds. He is not a hero in the proper sense of the word. He is helped all the time by the feminine element, which solves the whole problem for him and performs all the necessary deeds such as weaving the carpet and jumping through the ring. The story ends with a marriage—a balanced union of the male and female elements. So the general structure seems to point to a problem in which there is a dominating male attitude, a situation which lacks the feminine element, and the story tells us how the missing feminine is brought up and restored.

We have first to take the symbolism of the king. An expanded study of the king in alchemy is to be found in the section headed "Rex and Regina" in Jung's *Mysterium Coniunctionis*.[24] Jung brings in much other material, but I shall now only briefly condense what he says about the king.

In primitive societies the king or the chief of the tribe generally has magical qualities; he has mana. Certain chiefs, for instance, are so sacred that they may not touch the earth and are always carried by their people. In other tribes the vessels that the king has used for eating and drinking are thrown away and nobody may touch them; they are taboo. Some chiefs and kings are never seen because of a similar taboo; if you were to look at the king's face, you would die. Of certain chiefs it is said that their voices thunder and their eyes emanate lightning. In many primitive societies, the prosperity of the whole country depends on the health and state of mind of the king, and if he becomes impotent or ill, he has to be killed and replaced by another king whose health and potency guarantee the fertility of the women and cattle as well as the prosperity of the whole tribe. Frazer mentions instances in which it is not customary to wait until the king becomes impotent or sick but instead he is killed at the end of a certain period—say, after five, ten, or fifteen years—with the same idea in mind: namely, that he is worn out periodically and must be replaced. In certain tribes the idea prevails that this means not really killing the king, who embodies a kind of protective or ancestral spirit for the tribe, but simply a change of location: the old house is pulled down so that the spirit can move into a new one and continue to reign in that. It is believed to be always the same sacred, totemistic spirit that rules, and the killing of the king provides it with a better physical vessel.

We can say, therefore, that the king or chief incorporates a divine principle on which the entire welfare—psychic and physical—of the nation depends. He represents the divine principle in its visible form; he is its incarnation or embodiment, its dwelling place. In his body lives the totem spirit of the tribe. He therefore has many characteristics that would incline us to look at him as a symbol of the Self, because the Self, according to our definition, is the center of the self-regulating system of the psyche, on which the welfare of the individual depends. (Our own kings often held the sphere of the earth-ball, with the cross on it if the king was a Christian, and they carried a number of other symbols which we know from various mythological setups represent the Self.)

In many tribes there is a split between medicine man and king or chief—that is, between spiritual and worldly power—and the same thing happened in our civilization in the terrible fight between *sacerdotium* and *imperium* (church and state) in the Middle Ages. Both these powers claimed to be visible, incarnate symbols of the divine principle for their subjects—or, one could say, symbols of the unobservable archetype of the Self.

In all countries and in alchemical symbolism, which you can read about in Jung's book, you see this dominating idea that the aging king is unsatisfactory in some way. In primitive tribes, when he is impotent, the harem whispers that around and the tribe silently decides to kill him. Or he may be unsatisfactory in other ways: he may be too old to perform certain tasks any longer, or his time is over—he has reigned his ten or fifteen years. Then comes the inevitable idea of the king's sacrificial death.

In more advanced civilizations, as, for instance, in the Old Kingdom of Egypt, the practice was replaced by a ritual of renewal, a symbolic death and resurrection of the king, as was performed in the Sed festival. In other countries there was a so-called carnival king. Some criminal who had been condemned to death was allowed to live for three days as a king. He was clothed as a king, had all the insignia, was taken out of prison, and could order whatever he liked. He could have all the women he wanted, all the good dinners he liked, and everything else, and after three days he was executed. There are other rituals where the process of killing is carried out on a puppet which is "killed" instead of the king. Behind these different traditions we see the same motif—that of the necessity for the king to be renewed through death and rebirth.

If you apply that to our hypothesis that the king is a symbol of the Self, you have to ask: why does a symbol of the Self age? Do we know any psychological factors that correspond to this fact? If you study the comparative history of religions, you will note the tendency for any religious ritual or dogma that has become conscious to wear out after a time, to lose its original emotional impact and become a dead formula. Although it also acquires the positive qualities of consciousness, such as continuity, it loses the irrational contact with the flow of life and tends to become mechanical. This is true not only of religious doctrines and political systems but for everything else as well, because when something has long been conscious, the wine goes out of the bottle. It becomes a dead world. Therefore, if our conscious life is to avoid petrifaction, there is a necessity for constant renewal by contact with the flow of psychic events in the unconscious, and the king, being the dominant and most central symbol in the contents of the collective unconscious, is naturally subject to this need to an even greater extent.

You can therefore say that the symbol of the Self is especially exposed to this general difficulty of needing the constant renewal of understanding and contact, that it is especially threatened by the possibility of becoming a dead formula—a system and doctrine emptied of its meaning and therefore purely an outer form. In that sense we can say that the aging king represents a dominant content of collective consciousness and underlies all the political and religious doctrines of a social group. In the East, for many layers of the population, this content appeared as the Buddha, and with us, until now, it was Christ, who actually has the title King of Kings.

In our story the king apparently has no wife, or, if he has one, she does not appear. What would the queen represent? If we take the king as representing a central and dominant symbolic content of collective consciousness, then the queen would be its accompanying feminine element—the emotions, feelings, the irrational attachments to this dominant content. It can be said that in every civilization there is a *Weltanschauung* with a central God-image which dominates that civilization, and with that goes a certain habit or style of life, a feeling style, and that Eros style in society influences how people relate to one another. The feeling tone of this collectivity would be the queen who accompanies the king; for instance, in the Middle Ages the Gothic idea of Christ would be incarnate in the king of that time, while the representations of Eros—to be found in the poems of the Troubadours—would be manifested in the Virgin Mary, who is the Queen of Heaven related to the King—Christ. She set the pattern for feminine behavior, the pattern for the man's anima as well as for women. In Catholic countries women still naturally tend to adapt to that pattern, and men try to educate their anima to fit into this style of erotic behavior and this style of relationship.

So you see the close connection between the king and the queen, the Logos principle dominating a certain civilization and collective attitude, and the Eros style accompanying it in a specific form. That the queen is lacking means that the latter aspect has been lost and therefore the king is sterile. Without the queen he can have no more children. We must assume, therefore, that the story has to do with the problem of a dominant collective attitude in which the principle of Eros—of relatedness to the unconscious, to the irrational, the feminine—has been lost. This must refer to a situation where collective consciousness has become petrified and has stiffened into doctrines and formulas.

Now this king has three sons, so there is the problem of four males, three of whom are adapted in the way they should be while the fourth is below the mark. Naturally, people who know Jungian psychology will jump to the conclusion that those are obviously the four functions of consciousness: the king being the dominant or main function and the two elder sons being the auxiliary functions, while Dummling would be of course the fourth, inferior function. This is right, but only with a grain of salt because Jung's theory of the four functions refers to an individual. In fairy tales we do not have the inner story of one individual and therefore cannot look at it from this angle. We have, rather, to amplify the motif of the male quaternio first and there we find—in past history, for instance— motifs such as the four sons of Horus, the four Evangelists, and other quaternios, surrounding a main symbol of the Self.

These quaternios to be found in the comparative history of religion and in mythology cannot, to my mind, be interpreted as the four functions as they appear in an individual. They represent a more basic pattern of consciousness, from which the four-functional pattern of consciousness is derived. If we know how to diagnose a type and have a number of people before us, we can say that this man is a thinking type and his inferior feeling probably makes such and such trouble. Thus you can say that certain aspects of the setup are typical, while others are more individual. So it can be said that the problem of the four functions always appears in an individual in a certain setup, but that there are general basic trends underneath. Finally, if you want to puzzle, you say: why on earth does human consciousness tend always to develop four functions in each person? And there you can reply that it seems to be an inborn disposition of the human being to build up a four-functional conscious system. If you do not influence a child, he or she will automatically develop one conscious function, and if you analyze that person at the age of thirty or forty, you will find this four-functional structure. The underlying general disposition is mirrored in the many quaternarian symbols in mythology, such as the four winds, the four directions of the compass, and also these four royal figures in our fairy tale.

To be accurate you would therefore say that the king does not represent the main function but is the archetypal basis of that function in the sense that he is that psychological factor which builds up the main functions in all people. Now you will say that I am contradicting myself, for first I said that the old king was the dominant of collective consciousness and now I say that he symbolizes that disposition which builds up main functions. How does that link up? Is that a contradiction? This seems to be a second interpretation, but if you reflect on how a main function builds up, then you will see that it builds up in the first half of human life and generally serves collective adaptation. If a child is good at playing with practical things, his father will say that he will be an engineer later, and the child is encouraged, and at school he will be very good in those fields and very bad in others; so he will be proud of what he can do well and will do that most, because there is a natural tendency to do always what one can do well and to neglect the other side. This one-sidedness slowly builds up the main function, which is that function with which one adapts to collective requirements. Hence the dominant of collective consciousness also constellates in the individual the main function.

Take again the medieval man, for whom the dominant of the Self is the figure of Christ. If he has the disposition to become a thinking type, he will meditate with his thinking about the essence of Christ; if his inborn tendency is to become a feeling type, he will be moved by the prayers he hears and will not think about the symbol of Christ but will relate to him with his main function, feeling. That, therefore, is how the king represents the dominating symbolic content of a collective-conscious situation, and will also be connected with the main function in all people.

Now the other sons would therefore logically have to be interpreted along the same lines: that is, the two sons who are intelligent and clever would represent the typical basis for building up the two auxiliary functions in a human being, and Dummling would represent the basis of building up the inferior function. But Dummling is not only this; he is also the hero, and the whole story is concerned with what happens to him. We must therefore discuss briefly what the hero means in a mythological story, because if you read many psychological interpretations of myths, you will soon see that there is a constant shift between interpreting the hero as a symbol of the Self and as a symbol of the ego. Even the same interpreters contradict themselves within the same text. They begin as if the hero were an ego, then shift to his being the Self.

Before we discuss this problem, we have to be clear as to what we mean by ego. The ego is the central complex of the field of consciousness of the personality. But then, naturally, all other people have an ego too, so you can see that if we speak of *the* ego, that is already an abstraction, for we mean by that the "I" of all the people we know. If we repeat such a sentence as "The ego resists the unconscious," then we make a general observation, something which applies on an average ego, stripped of all more subjective and unique qualities.

We now have to look at the symbol of the hero in myths. What does he usually do? He is very often a savior: he saves his country and his people from dragons, witches, and evil spells. In many stories he is the finder of the hidden treasure. He frees his tribe and leads them out of all sorts of dangers. He reconnects his people with the gods and with life, or he renews the life principle. It is he who goes on the night-sea journey, and when he comes out of the belly of the whale, with him generally come all those who were swallowed before him. Sometimes he is likely to be overly self-confident and in certain myths destructive. Then the gods, or some enemy powers, decide to destroy him. In many hero myths he is also the innocent victim of evil powers. Then there is the hero-trickster figure, who plays good and bad tricks and who not only frees his people but at the same time gets them into difficulties; he helps certain people and destroys others by mistake or by thoughtlessness, so he is half a devil and half a savior, and again he is either destroyed, reformed, or transformed at the end of the story.

Thus among the hero figures there is a great variety: the Dummling type; the trickster type; the strong man type; the innocent, beautiful youth type; the sorcerer type; the one who performs his deeds by magic, or by power and courage. We know from the investigations of child psychology that in the first twenty years of life, to take a broad estimate, the main tendency of the unconscious itself goes into building up a strong ego complex, and most of the early difficulties in youth result from disturbances of this process by negative parental influence or through some traumatic or other hindrance. In cases such as Michael Fordham has described in his publications, the ego complex is not capable of building itself up. But there are natural processes in the psyche of the child that we can watch, for they are mirrored in dreams, in which you can see how the ego builds up. One way, which one sees frequently, is in the ideal of the model hero. Papa often fills this role, as do tram conductors, policemen, elder brothers, or big boys in the class above at school, who receive the child's transference. In secret daydreams the child imagines that that is what he would like to become. The fantasies of many little boys are of wearing a red cap and waving the trains on and off, of being the chief, the big boss, the king, and the chief of police. These model figures are projections produced by the unconscious; they either appear immediately in the dreams of young people or are projected onto outer figures, and they catch the fantasy of the child and influence his ego buildup. Every mother knows that. For instance, if you take a little boy to the dentist, then you say, 'Well, you are the chief of police, so you can't cry when a tooth is pulled out!' That strengthens his ego so that he will force back his tears. That method is constantly employed in education; it is a trick. If a boy admires Albert in the next class and behaves badly, you say, "Albert wouldn't do that," and the boy at once pulls up his socks.

Those are typical psychological processes showing how in a young person the ego complex, the center of the field of consciousness, is slowly formed. If you look more closely at these processes, you will see from dreams that they stem from the Self and that it is the Self which builds up the ego. A graphic representation would show first the unknown psychic totality of a human being—thought of as a sphere, not a circle—and then in the upper part of the sphere could be the field of consciousness; anything within this field is conscious to me. The center is the ego complex. What is not connected through some thread of association with my ego complex is unconscious to me. Before this field of consciousness exists, the self-regulating center (the Self is regarded as the totality and the regulating center of the whole personality, and it seems to be present from the very beginning of life) builds up the ego complex through certain emotional and other processes. If you study the symbolism of the ego complex and of the Self, you will see that the ego has the same structures and is to a great extent a mirror image of this center. We know the representations of the Self in mandala construction, for instance; the ego has the same fourfold subdivision. The center of the Self slowly builds up the ego complex, which then mirrors its original center and which, as we all know, often succumbs to the illusion of being that center. Most people who are not analyzed naturally believe—because of their emotional conviction that "I am I"—that "I" am the whole thing; and even that illusion comes from the ego's having been formed from the total center. But in childhood there is the tragedy of separation; there is, for instance, the typical event of being thrown out of Paradise, of having one's first shock of incompleteness and discovering that something perfect has been forever lost. Such tragedies mirror the moment when the ego begins to become an entity apart from the Self. Then the ego is established as a self-existing factor, and the intuitive connection with the center is partly lost.

Now the ego, as far as we can see, functions properly only when it achieves a certain adaptation to the whole psyche, which means that it functions best if a certain plasticity is kept—in other words, when the ego is not petrified and therefore can, through dreams, moods, and so on, still be influenced by the Self so as to adapt to the whole psychological system. It looks to us as though the ego were meant by nature not to be a ruler of the whole psychological setup, but to be an instrument, which functions best if it still obeys the basic instinctual urges of the totality and does not resist them.

Imagine, for instance, that your instinct tells you to run away in a dangerous situation. (You do not require a very conscious ego to tell you that.) If a bull chases you, you do not need to consult your ego; you had better consult your legs, which know what to do. But if the ego functions *with* your legs, so that while running away from the bull you also look for a good hiding place or a fence to jump over, then the situation is perfect: your instincts and your ego function in accord with each other. If, on the other hand, you are a philosopher whose legs want to run away but who thinks: "Stop! I must first find out whether it is right to run away from a bull," then the ego blocks the instinctual urge; it has become autonomous and anti-instinctive and then becomes a destructive nuisance, such as we see in every neurotic individual. A neurosis could even be defined as an ego formation no longer in harmony with the whole personality, whereas when the ego functions in accordance with the larger totality, it reinforces itself and improves the innate cleverness of the basic instinctive arrangement.

Naturally sometimes the ego would also be useful in resisting instinct. Imagine, for instance, the North Arctic lemmings, which get an instinctual urge to make a migration into another country where they can start again with a new food supply. Driven by an instinctual urge, they collect together and then march on. If, by a piece of bad luck, they come to the sea or a river, they go into it and drown by the thousands. I am sure you know this story, which has always puzzled zoologists, for it shows the silly unadaptedness of some natural instincts. Konrad Lorenz once gave a lecture with many such examples; I remember one about a bird which, to please its mate in the mating season, produces an enormous red sack on his chest with which to enforce his mating song. This red sack is so heavy that he cannot fly, so his enemies gather and butcher that bird. So that is not a very good invention. A beautiful red tail or a red behind like a baboon's to please his wife would be much better and would not prevent him from flying away. So you see, instinctual patterns are not only positive. If a lemming could ask itself what it was doing and reflect that it did not want to drown, and could go back, that would be very useful for it. So that is probably why nature has invented the ego as a new instrument for us; we are a new experiment of nature, for we have an additional instrument for regulating the instinctual urges. We do not live only on our patterns of behavior but have this strange addition known as the ego.

The ideal situation, as far as we can see, is when the ego, with a certain plasticity, obeys the central regulation of the psyche. But when it hardens and becomes autonomous, acting according to its own reasons, then there is often a neurotic constellation. This happens not only to individuals, but also collectively, which is why we speak of collective neuroses and psychoses. Whole groups of mankind can drift into that split situation and deviate from their basic instinctual patterns, and then disaster is close. That is why in hero stories there is nearly always an exposition of a terrible situation: the land is drying up because the toads block the water of life, or some dark enemy comes from the north and steals all the women and there is no fertility in the land. Whatever this terrible story is, the hero has the task of putting it right. The dragon may be demanding all the king's maidens to be sacrificed. Everyone in the country is already wearing black, and now the last princess has to be given to the dragon—then always the hero comes.

The hero, therefore, is the restorer of a healthy, conscious situation. He is the one ego that restores to healthy, normal functioning a situation in which all the egos of that tribe or nation are deviating from their instinctive, basic totality pattern. It can therefore be said that *the hero is an archetypal figure which presents a model of an ego functioning in accord with the Self.* Produced by the unconscious psyche, it is a *model* to be looked at, and it is demonstrating a rightly functioning ego, an ego that functions in accordance with the requirements of the Self. That is why the hero seems, to a certain extent, to *be* the Self: because he serves as its instrument and completely expresses what the Self wants to have happen. In a way, therefore, he is also the Self, because he expresses or incarnates its healing tendencies. So the hero has this strange double character. From the feeling standpoint you can naively understand that. If you hear a hero myth, you identify with the hero and get infected by his mood. Let us say, for instance, that an Eskimo tribe is on the way to starvation. Caribou hunting has been bad, and primitives very easily give up and die from discouragement before it is physically or psychologically necessary. And then comes a storyteller and tells about a fellow who made contact with ghosts and by that saved his starving tribe, and so on. That puts them on their feet again, purely emotionally. The ego adopts a heroic, courageous, and hopeful attitude that saves the collective situation. That is why a hero story is a vital necessity in difficult life conditions. If you have your hero myth again, then you can live. It is something to live for. You are naturally encouraged by it.

When you tell fairy tales to children, they at once and naively identify and get all the feeling of the story. If you tell them about the poor little duck, all the children who have inferiority complexes hope that in the end they too will get a princess. That functions exactly as it should; it gives a model for living, an encouraging, vivifying model which reminds one unconsciously of all life's positive possibilities.

There is a beautiful custom among Australian aborigines: when the rice does not grow well, the women go into the rice field and squat among the rice and tell it the myth of the origin of the rice. Then the rice knows again why it is there and grows like anything. That is probably a projection of our own situation; for with us it is certainly true, for if we get those myths we think that now we know again what we are living for, and that changes our whole life-mood and can even sometimes change our physiological condition.

If you interpret the hero in this way, then you see why Dumm-ling would be the hero. Since the king is the dominant of the collective conscious attitude which has lost contact with the flow of life, especially with the feminine, the Eros principle, Dummling represents the new conscious attitude which is capable of contact-ing the feminine, for he is the one who brings up the toad-princess. Characteristically, he is the one who is called stupid and seemingly unlucky. But if you look at his behavior more closely, you see that he is simply spontaneous and naive; he takes things as they are. For instance, the two other brothers cannot accept facts. Each time Dummling wins, they want another competition, saying that that one was not right. But Dummling always simply does the next thing. When he has to marry a frog—well, that is not very pleasant, but that's how it is. Obviously, it is that quality which is empha-sized in our story.

We should always look at these stories as we do at the dreams of individuals and ask what conscious situation is compensated by such a myth. Then you clearly see that such a story compensates the conscious attitude of a society in which patriarchal schemes and oughts and shoulds dominate. It is ruled by rigid principles because of which the irrational, spontaneous adaptation to events is lost. It is typical that Dummling stories are statistically more frequent in the white man's society than in others, and it is obvious why that is so. We are the people who, by an overdevelopment of consciousness, have lost the flexibility of taking life as it is. That is why Dummling stories are especially valuable for us. We have also an overwhelming number of stories where the hero excels through just plain laziness; he simply sits on a stove and scratches himself, and then everything falls into his lap. These stories also compensate for the collective attitude which puts too much emphasis on efficiency: then those lazy hero stories are told and retold with great delight—and with a healing meaning in them.

Now the king does not know to whom he should leave the kingdom. There he deviates from his probable former behavior, for he leaves it to fate to settle who shall inherit the kingdom. This is not the general behavior. It is frequent in the case of the old king, but it is not the only possible one. There are, for instance, other stories where the old king has information—a dream perhaps, or a prophecy about who is to be the next king—and he puts all his passion and strength and skill into destroying his possible successor. That is another type of story. An example would be Grimms' "The Devil with the Three Golden Hairs," but there are thousands of them. Sometimes at the beginning of the story the king gives his possible successors a chance, but if a successor who does not suit his plans is chosen, then he begins to resist.

There are neurotic people whose ego attitude has derived from their whole psychological nature yet who come into analysis without great resistances, for they just want to know "What next?" and if their dreams produce some new life, they take it and go on, with practically no resistance. With them the "succession of the king"—one ego attitude replaced by another—is relatively easy. But there are others who describe their symptoms and you look at their dreams, but if you even mildly suggest what the trouble might be, they jump at your throat and argue that it may be anything else, but it is certainly not *that*. *That* they *know* is all right, and they fight back forever. This is the type of ego formation which has already stiffened to such an extent that it absolutely refuses the possibility of a renewal. I often say to such people that they have the attitude of a person who goes to a doctor and asks the doctor please to cure him—but not to examine the urine because that is something private. A lot of people do this. They go into analysis but keep the main information in their pockets because it is nobody's business to know about that. In all such variations of behavior you see the old king—which in an individual means the center of consciousness—resisting renewal.

Naturally, that is to be found in the collective situation as well. A whole society may first be violently antagonistic to some religious reform and afterward suddenly recognize it. To mention a classical example, twelve sentences written by Saint Thomas of Aquinas, the great pillar of the Catholic Church, were condemned by a Concilium in 1320. So you can see that through the collective prejudice of the time, something which is later recognized as not being inimical to the dominating attitude is at first resisted. That extends into political and religious persecution, newspaper pressure, and business persecution, and so on—all that is going on now and always will in social setups everywhere in the world. There is the phobia that something new is in itself terrifying. All that is typical behavior of the old king, and it can be stiffened into mistrust and real tragedy—or, as happens here, it need not become a tragedy. This story mirrors the possibility of a renewal occurring without any crisis or tragedy. It is a mild story, which is why it is not particularly interesting, but it has all the classical features we need.

We come next to the ritual of the three feathers. This general custom of the time is not very different from throwing a coin. Whenever consciousness cannot decide rationally, one can have recourse to such a chance event and take that as an indication. That the coin falls this way or the wind blows that way is a "just-so" story taken as a meaningful hint. This in itself is important because it is the first move toward giving up ego determination, one's own conscious reasoning. One could say that this old king proves to be not too bad because, though he will soon be dead and therefore has to be replaced by a successor, he is quite willing to leave it to the gods to decide who shall come next. It again fits the whole setup of the story, which is not dramatic and which has not stiffened into a conflict.

To carry the symbolism further: in mythology, feathers generally represent something very similar to the bearer of the feathers—the bird. According to the principle of *pars pro toto* (the part stands for the whole), a magical form of thinking, the feather signifies the bird, and birds in general represent psychic entities of an intuitive and thinking character. For instance, the soul of the dead leaves the dying body in the form of a bird. There are medieval representations of this. In certain villages of Upper Wallis even today, in every house, in the parents' bedroom, there is a little window called the soul window, which is opened only when someone is dying, so that the soul can leave through it. The idea is that the soul, a fluttering being, goes out like a bird escaping from its cage. In *The Odyssey* Hermes gathers the souls of Ulysses' enemies, and they chatter like birds (the Greek word is *thrizein*) and follow him with wings like bats'. Also, in the underworld where Enkidu, the friend of Gilgamesh, goes, the dead sit around in the feather garments of birds. So birds, you could say, stand for a nearly bodiless entity, an inhabitant of the air, of the wind sphere, which has always been associated with breath and therefore with the human psyche. Therefore, especially in the stories of North and South American Indians, where it is used very often, one meets the idea that gluing feathers to an object means that it is psychically real. There is even a South American tribe which uses the word for feather as a suffix to describe something which only exists psychologically and not in outer reality. You can speak of a fox-feather, an arrow-feather, or a tree-feather, the word *feather* indicating that the fox or the arrow or the tree is not contained in physical reality but has to do with psychic reality. When North American Indians and certain Eskimo tribes send messengers inviting others to a religious festival, the messengers carry sticks with feathers on them, the feathers making the bearer sacrosanct. Because they carry a spiritual message, such messengers may not be killed. By attaching feathers to himself, the primitive marks himself as a psychic and spiritual being.

Since the feather is very light, every breath of wind carries it. It is that which is very sensitive to what one could call invisible and imperceptible psychological spiritual currents. Wind, in most religious and mythological connections, represents spiritual power, which is why we use the word *inspiration*. In the Whitsun miracle the Holy Ghost filled the house like a wind; spirits make a kind of cold wind when they come, and the appearance of ghosts is generally accompanied by breathings or currents of wind. The word *spiritus* is connected with *spirare* (to breathe). In Genesis the *Ruach Elohim* (the Spirit of God) broods over the waters. Therefore you can say that an imperceptible wind whose direction you can only discover by blowing a feather would be a slight, barely noticeable, almost inconceivable psychic tendency—a final tendency in the current psychological flow of life.

That is what happens when someone comes into analysis and tells you all his troubles and you say, "Well, I am not more intelligent than you. I do not see through this, but let us look at what the dreams say." And then we look at them from a final angle; we look to see where the current in the dreams seems to point. According to the Jungian point of view, they are not only causal but also have a final aspect and we therefore look to see where the libido tends to go. We "throw a feather in the air" and look to see the direction it takes, and then say, "Let's go that way because there is a slight tendency in that direction."

That is what the king does; he makes himself completely flexible and consults the supernatural powers. One feather goes to the east, the other to the west, and Dummling's feather settles on the ground right away. According to some more witty variations, it settles on a brown stone just in front of him, and then Dummling says: "Well, that means I can go nowhere"—and then finds a stair leading into the earth, which is in beautiful accord with his character. Very often we look God-knows-where for the solution of our problem and do not see that it is right in front of our noses. We are not humble enough to look downward but stick our noses up in the air. That is why Jung often told the beautiful story of a Jewish rabbi who was asked by his pupils why in the Bible there were so many instances of the apparition of God, whereas nowadays such things did not happen, and the rabbi replied, "Because nowadays nobody is humble enough to bend down low enough." But Dummling, because he is naive and unsophisticated, has a naive and unsophisticated attitude toward life. He is naturally led to what is right on the ground and right in front of his nose—and there it is. We know from the first sentence of the story that it is the feminine which is lacking, so naturally it is found in the earth and nowhere else. That belongs to the inner logic of the whole story.

5

"THE THREE FEATHERS"
CONTINUED

Although we have amplified the three-feathers motif, we have not
yet taken the second step of expressing its psychological meaning
in a nutshell. Feathers represent thoughts or fantasies; they replace,
pars pro toto, birds, and the wind is a well-known symbol for the
inspiring spiritual quality of the unconscious. So this motif would
mean that one lets one's imagination or thoughts wander, following
the inspirations which well up from the unconscious. You might
perform this ritual if you were at a crossroads and did not know
what direction to take. Instead of deciding out of ego considera-
tions, you wait for a hunch from the unconscious and let it have a
say in the matter. We could understand that as a compensation for
the dominant collective situation, which seems to have lost contact
with the irrational, feminine element. If a single man or if a whole
civilization loses contact with the feminine element, that usually
implies a too rational, too ordered, too organized attitude. Along
with the feminine go the feeling, the irrational, and fantasy, and
here, instead of telling the sons where to go, this old king makes a
gesture toward possible renewal by allowing the wind to tell them.
Dummling's feather falls straight ahead of him onto the ground,
where he discovers a trapdoor with steps beneath it leading into
the depths of Mother Earth. In the Hessian parallel, the frog prin-

cess tells him that he should *sich versenken*—he should go into the depths. Always the downward movement is emphasized.

If there is a trapdoor and then steps leading into the earth, it is not the same as if there were just a natural cavity. Here, human beings have left their traces; perhaps there has been a building, or perhaps this is the cellar of a castle of which the upper part has long ago disappeared, or it was once a hiding place in a former civilization. Often when figures go down into the earth or into the water in a dream, people superficially interpret that as a *descensus ad inferos,* as a descent into the underworld, into the depths of the unconscious. But one should see whether it is a descent into unconscious virginal nature or whether there are layers and traces of former civilizations. The latter would indicate that there were elements which had once been conscious, but which had sunk back into the unconscious, just as a castle may fall into ruins but its cellars remain, leaving traces of a former way of life.

Interpreted psychologically, this would mean that the unconscious not only contains our instinctive animal nature but also contains the traditions of the past and is partially formed by them. This is why in analysis, elements of an earlier civilized past frequently reappear. A Jew may not care in the least about his cultural past, but kabbalistic motifs appear in his dreams. We once saw the dreams of a Hindu who had been educated in America and who consciously had not the slightest interest in his cultural past, but his dreams were full of Hindu godheads still alive in his unconscious. It has often been erroneously believed that Jung had a tendency to force people back into their cultural background; for instance, that he insisted that Jews should again dig up Orthodox symbolism or that Hindus should again pray to Shiva. This is not at all the case. There is absolutely no "should" or "ought" about it; it is simply a question whether such elements come up and want to be recognized in this person's unconscious or not.

How can it be that in our story the feminine element was at one time more conscious and has now sunk back into the unconscious? The original pagan Germanic and Celtic religions had many cults of Mother Earth and other nature goddesses, but the one-sided patriarchal superstructure of the Christian civilization slowly repressed this element. Naturally, therefore, if there is a question of bringing up the feminine element and integrating it again, we shall (at least in Europe) find traces of a past civilization in which it was much more conscious. In the Middle Ages with the cult of the Virgin Mary and the Troubadours, the recognition of the anima was much more alive than it was from the sixteenth century onward, a time which is characterized by an increasing repression of the feminine element and of Eros culture in our part of the world. We do not know the date of this fairy tale, but the opening situation shows a condition where the feminine element is not recognized, though obviously it had been at one time, which is why there is an easy possibility of getting back to it. Dummling can go down into the earth step by step and does not fall headlong or get lost in the dark. (In the Hessian parallel the steps have a round cover with a ring in it, like the rings on the covers of manholes in the street, so there is an allusion not only to the symbol of the anima but to the Self.)

When Dummling goes down, he finds a door and knocks at it, and he hears that strange little poem.

> *Virgin, green and small,*
> *Shrivel leg,*
> *Shrivel leg's dog,*
> *Shrivel back and forth.*
> *Let's see who is outside.*

It is a kind of childish ditty with only a partly understandable, dreamlike combination of words. When the door opens, Dummling sees an enormous toad surrounded by a circle of little toads, and when he says he wants a beautiful carpet, they produce it out of the box.

We have first to amplify the poem and mainly the symbol of the toad. In many other variations of this fairy tale, the toad is replaced by a frog, so we have to look at the frog as well. In general, the frog in mythology is often a masculine element, whereas the toad is feminine. In Europe there is the frog prince, and in African and Malayan stories the frog is also a male being, while in practically all other civilizations the toad is feminine. In China a three-legged toad lives in the moon and together with a hare produces the elixir of life. According to a Taoist tradition she has been fished up from the "well of truth" and as a kind of protecting spirit works with the hare to make the elixir pills which heal and prolong life. In our civilization, the toad has always been associated with the Earth Mother, especially in her function of helping at childbirth. She was looked on, and is even now regarded, as being a representation of the uterus. In Catholic countries, after a leg or a hand or some other part has been cured by a saint, a wax image is made of the injured part and suspended as an *ex voto* (a token of the fulfill-ment of one's vow) at the church where healing was requested. Now if a woman has a disease of the uterus or some trouble connected with childbirth, she will not make a wax image of her uterus but will suspend a wax toad in the church, for the toad represents the uterus. In many churches and chapels in Bavaria, the statue of the Virgin is surrounded by such toads made out of wax. There the Virgin Mary has taken over the function of the Greek goddess Artemis Eileithyia, the helper in birth, the positive mother who helps the woman carry the child and give birth to it without harm. This analogy of toad and uterus shows how much the toad in this connection actually represents the maternal womb, the mother—just that which is lacking in the royal family.

The big toad in the middle could be looked upon as the mother of all the little toads sitting around her. Our Dummling does not marry the big toad; he takes one of the little ones out of the ring and she turns into the beautiful princess, which shows even more clearly that the big toad is the mother figure from whose circle he gets his anima. For, as we know, the anima is a derivative of the mother image in a man's psychology. Here the Mother Earth goddess is really in the center. The word *shrivel* is rather more difficult to understand. Certainly in the German language *hutzel*, the original word, is always associated with old age, ancientness, something which has lasted for a long time. It could allude to the fact that the Mother Goddess has been excluded from the realm of consciousness and neglected and has thus shriveled up in the cellar like an old apple.

Now we come to the leg (*Bein*), which I am inclined to interpret rather as a bone (also *Bein* in German) than as a leg because of a widespread ritual for a love charm in German, Swiss, and Austrian countries, according to which a man must take a toad or a frog and throw it alive into an ant heap. Then he must run away and not listen because the toad or frog might cry and that would mean that he was cursed by it. The ants will then eat the toad or frog until only the bones are left; then the man must take one of the leg bones and keep it, and if he secretly touches a woman's back with it without her noticing it, she will fall hopelessly in love with him. Thus toads and frogs are very much used in witchcraft and magic for love charms and aphrodisiac potions. Also in folklore the poisonous nature of the toad is very much emphasized. Actually a toad, if touched, exudes a liquid which, though not dangerous to humans, can cause an eczema, a slight inflammation of the skin. Smaller animals can be killed by this exudation. Since in folklore this fact is much exaggerated, the toad is looked upon as a witch animal, and its pulverized skin and legs are used as one of the basic ingredients of practically all witch potions.

To sum up, we see that the toad is an earth goddess which has power over life and death: it can poison or it can bring life, and it has to do with the love principle. Thus the toad really contains all the elements lacking in the conscious setup of our story. It is green, the color of vegetation and nature, and a third line in the verse speaks of *Hutzelbeins Hündchen*—Shrivel leg's little dog. So there is a strange kind of association with a little dog, which is not quite clear but becomes clearer if you look up Bolte and Polivka's collection of parallels, where you will find that in many other versions, particularly in many French parallels, the redeemed princess is not a toad but a little dog. Obviously there is a shifting or intermingling of motifs, for sometimes it is a little white dog and sometimes either a cat, a mouse, or a toad. Should the bewitched or unredeemed princess be a little dog, she would naturally be much closer to the human realm than a frog; she would have been neglected and have regressed to an unconscious level, but she would be less low and less far away than if she had regressed to the level of a toad or a frog. So we could say that Dummling finds the lacking feminine element in a nonhuman form, as a cold-blooded animal or, if a dog, in the form of a warm-blooded animal.

The formation of this big toad with a ring of little toads at the entrance, in that other parallel, also shows that together with the feminine, the symbol of totality is constellated.

We now have to go into the symbolism of the carpet. In European civilization the carpet was not known until we came into contact with the East. The nomadic Arab tribes, who are still famous for their carpet weaving, say that the carpets they use in their tents represent that continuity of earth which they need to prevent them from feeling that they have no soil under their feet. Wherever they go, they first spread one of those beautiful carpets with its usually sacred pattern, and over that they put the tent. It is the basis on which they stand, as we do on our earth. It also protects them from the evil influences of a foreign soil.

All the higher warm-blooded animals, including ourselves, have a strong attachment to their own territories. Most animals have an instinct to have and to defend a territory. We know that animals return to their territories. Efforts have been made to exile mice miles from their homes, but they walk back through all the dangers and difficulties, and only when the chance of survival is nil does the mouse not return but tries to get a new territory by fighting and driving out another mouse. In its own territory an animal has a kind of quick, intimate knowledge of the whole situation, so that when an enemy comes it can hide at once, whereas if it sees the shadow of a hawk in a strange territory, it has to look around to find a place to hide and may lose just that second required for its escape. Heinrich Hediger, a professor of zoology at Zürich University, has gone further into these problems and has tried to establish the fact that the territorial instinct in animals is derived from the mother attachment. He claims that the original territory of every young animal is its mother's body; the young animal grows in and lives on the mother's body, the clearest example being the kangaroo. This instinct is later transferred from the mother's body to the territory. We know that when animals are caught and transported, they make a home territory of their transport cage, and if that is destroyed and they are put into a new home right away, they may die. The transport box, with the animal in it, must always be put into the new place so that the animal can slowly acclimatize itself to its new home, after which the transport cage can be removed. It is again the mother's womb, a habitat with a maternal quality, the feeling of which is slowly transferred onto the new territory.

We are just the same. If you cut off elderly people from their roots or make them move their homes, they often die. Many cling in an absolutely amazing way to their territory, and if you have ever watched your own dreams during a move, you will know that psychological upsets happen in your own psyche. Women, especially, suffer tremendously when they lose their territory, which is why Jung once said that he felt sorry for American women because of the moving from one place to another which is usual for them. Men can stand that much better because they have a more roaming tendency, but for a woman it is really difficult. To us too the territory means the mother, and for some of those North African nomadic tribes the carpet is that same thing, for they need the continuity of the maternal soil; and now having it outwardly, living practically every night on a different bit of sand, they carry their symbolic territory with them.

Now Islamic people, like the Jews, may not make an image of their Godhead, so the elements in carpets are mostly abstract designs which have a symbolic meaning. Most of them are motifs of the gazelle, of the camel, of the tree of life of Paradise, of a lamp, and so on, which have been transformed into purely geometrical designs. Carpet specialists are still able to say this is a lamp and that is really a gazelle, transformed into a pattern. Most of the elements in Oriental carpets refer to religious ideas: the lamp refers to illumination through Allah's wisdom, and the gazelle represents the human soul seeking for the Godhead. So the carpet represents not only Mother Earth for those people but also the inner basis of their whole life. Carpets very often appear in this way in the dreams of modern people. There is also the quotation from Faust, spoken by the spirit who visits Faust at the beginning of part one:

> So schaff ich am sausenden Webstuhl der Zeit
> Und wirke der Gottheit lebendiges Kleid.

> Thus at Time's whirling loom I ply
> And weave the vesture of God.

I think Goethe got this motif from Pherekydes' creation myth, which speaks of the earth as an enormous sort of cloak with woven patterns in it, spread over a world oak.

From these amplifications, you see that the woven cloak or carpet with its designs is often used as a symbol for the complex symbolic patterns of life and the secret designs of fate. It represents the greater pattern of our life, which we do not know as long as we live it. We constantly build our lives by our ego decisions, and it is only in old age when one looks back that one sees that the whole thing had a pattern. Some people who are more introspective know it a bit before the end of their lives and are secretly convinced that things have a pattern, that they are led, and that there is a kind of secret design behind the ephemeral actions and decisions of a human being. Actually, we turn toward dreams and the unconscious because we want to find out more about our life pattern in order to make fewer mistakes and not to cut with our knives into our own inner carpet, but to fulfill our destiny instead of resisting it. This purposiveness of an individual life pattern, which gives one a feeling of meaningfulness, is very often symbolized in the carpet. Generally carpets, especially Oriental ones, have those complicated meandering patterns such as you follow up when in a dreamy mood, when you feel that life goes up and down and along and changes around. Only if you look from afar, from a certain objective distance, do you realize that there is a pattern of wholeness in it.

Therefore, it is not off the point if, along with the forgotten feminine principles, there are no longer good carpets at the king's court and they need one, for they have again to find the pattern of life. In this way the story tells us that the subtlety of the inventions of the unconscious and the secret design woven into a human life are infinitely more intelligent than human consciousness—and more subtle and superior than man could invent. One is again and again overwhelmed by the genius of that unknown mysterious something in our psyche which is the inventor of our dreams. It picks elements from day impressions, from something the dreamer has read the evening before in the paper, or from a childhood memory, and makes a nice kind of potpourri out of it, and only when you have interpreted its meaning do you see the subtlety and the genius of each dream composition. Every night we have that carpet weaver at work within us, who makes those fantastically subtle patterns, so subtle that, unfortunately often after an hour's attempt to interpret them, we are unable to find out the meaning. We are just too clumsy and stupid to follow up the genius of that unknown spirit of the unconscious which invents dreams. But we can understand that this carpet is more subtly woven than any human could ever achieve.

Naturally this first test is not accepted by the king and the two elder brothers, and so the second time they have to find the most beautiful ring. There again the ritual of the three feathers follows and the elder brothers bring an ordinary iron cartwheel with its nails pulled out, being too lazy to look for anything better, while Dummling goes down to the toad and gets a beautiful gold ring shining with diamonds and precious stones.

The ring, as a circular object, is obviously one of the many symbols of the Self. But in the fairy tale there are so many symbols of the Self that we have to find out what specific function of the Self is stressed in this particular symbol. Now we know that the Self, being the central regulating factor of the unconscious psyche, has an enormous number of different functional aspects. It preserves the balance or, as we saw before with the hero symbol, it builds up an ego attitude in the right balance with the Self. The symbol of a ball would represent more the capacity of the Self to effect movement out of itself. For the primitive mind the ball was obviously that object with an amazing propensity for moving along on its own volition. So the primitive might suppress that little factor that an initial push is needed, since for him the ball becomes that thing which can move without outside impetus, of its own accord; by its own inner life-impulse it moves and keeps moving through all the vicissitudes and frictions and difficulties of the material world. Therefore, it stands for this very factor in the unconscious psyche, which Jung has discovered; namely, that the unconscious psyche has a capacity for creating movement born out of itself. It is not a system which reacts only to already existing outer factors but can, without traceable causal impulse, produce something new out of itself. It has a capacity for spontaneous movement, which in many philosophies and religious systems is otherwise only attributed to the Divinity, the first mover.

The psyche has something of this in itself as well; thus, for instance, we can analyze someone for a long time and the dreams seem to discuss certain obvious life problems and the person feels all right, but suddenly he will have a dream out of the blue which starts something completely new. A new creative idea which one could not expect or explain causally has arisen, as if the psyche had decided to bring up something new, and these are the great and meaningful healing psychological events. The symbol of the sphere or the ball (remember that spheres or balls or rolling apples very often replace feathers in our tale) primarily means this. That is why so often in fairy tales the hero follows a rolling apple or a rolling sphere to some mysterious goal. He just follows this spontaneous self-impulsiveness of his own psyche to the secret goal. (I have amplified the symbol of the ball in order to show its difference from the ring and to show that to say "a symbol of the Self" is not specific enough, but that you have always to go into the particular function of each Self symbol.)

The ring has in general two functions besides its quality of roundness, which makes it an image of the Self. It symbolizes either a connection or a fetter. The marriage ring, for instance, can mean connectedness with the partner, but it can also be a fetter—which is why some people take it off and put it in their pocket when they go traveling! So it depends on your own feeling toward it, whether it is a fetter or a meaningful connection. If a man gives a ring to a woman, he expresses, whether he knows it or not, the wish to be connected with her in a suprapersonal way, to be connected with her not just in an ephemeral love affair. He wants to say, "This is forever. It is eternal." And that means a connection via the Self, not only via ego-moods. Thus in the Catholic world marriage is a sacrament, and the connection is not only that of two egos making up their minds to have, as Jung expressed it, "a little financial society for the bringing up of children." If a marriage is more than that, it means the recognition that something suprapersonal, or, in religious language, divine enters into it and that it is meant forever in a much deeper sense than just the love mood or some calculation which brings people first together. The ring expresses an eternal connection through the Self, and whenever an analyst has to cope with marriage troubles or to accompany a human being on the last terrifying steps to the guillotine of his wedding day, very interesting dreams often point in this direction—that the marriage has to be made for the sake of individuation. That gives you a profoundly different basic attitude toward the everyday troubles which may arise. One knows that for better or worse, it is the fate by which one has to work through to higher consciousness and that one cannot just throw one's marriage over the first time something upsets one. That is secretly expressed by the wedding ring, which symbolizes a connection through the Self.

In general the ring means any kind of connectedness, and therefore it sometimes has quite a different aspect. Before performing many religious rituals, people must take off their rings. No Roman or Greek priest was allowed to perform any sacramental act without first removing all his rings. There it meant that he had to connect with the Godhead and therefore must put aside all other connections; he must strip himself of all other obligations so that he may be open only to the divine influence. In this sense the image of the ring stands—very often negatively in mythology—for being tied to something to which one should not be tied, being enslaved by some negative factor such as, for instance, a demon. In psychological language that would symbolize a state of being fascinated and being the slave of some emotional unconscious complex.

In amplifying the ring symbolism, we could pull in not only the ring for the finger but all other rings, such as a witch's ring or marching in a ring to carrying a hoop. In general the ring in this wider sense has the meaning of what Jung describes as a temenos, the sacred space set apart either by circumambulation or by drawing a circle. In Greece, a temenos was simply a small sacred place in a wood or on a hill, into which one might not enter without certain precautions, a place where people could not be killed. If one who was persecuted took refuge in a temenos, he could be neither captured nor killed while there. A temenos is an asylum, and within it one is *asulos* (inviolable). As a place of the cult of the god, it signifies the territory that belongs to the Godhead. Witches' rings have a similar meaning; they are a piece of earth marked off, a round place reserved for a numinous, archetypal purpose. Such a place has the double function of protection for what is within and exclusion of what is without, and of concentration on what is within. That is the general meaning which is to be found in so many forms. The word *temenos* comes from *temno,* to cut. It indicates being cut out from the meaningless, profane layer of life—a part cut out and isolated for a special purpose. But I do not think this is particularly relevant to our story, in which we have a finger ring.

The ring in our story is golden. Gold, as a most precious metal, has always in the planetary system been ascribed to the sun and is generally associated with incorruptibility and immortality. It is everlasting and in former times was the only known metal which did not decay or become black or green and resisted all corrosive elements. Gold treasures can be buried in the earth and dug up unharmed after a thousand years, unlike copper or silver or iron, so it is the immortal, the transcendental element, that which outlasts ephemeral existence; it is the eternal, the divine, and the most precious, and whenever something is made of gold, it is said to have that eternal quality. That is why a wedding ring is made of gold, for it is meant to last forever; it should not be corrupted by any negative earthly influences, and the precious stones emphasize this even more. Precious stones generally symbolize psychological values.

The old king and the two elder brothers at the king's court will not accept the fact that the youngest son has won this test again, so a third test is set. Now the kingdom will belong to the one who brings home the most beautiful wife. Dummling goes down to his toad, and this time the toad is not quite so ready to help. She says, "Well, well, the most beautiful wife! That is not at hand just now, but you shall have her!" So it seems to be a little bit more difficult this time, and she gives him a yellow carrot shaped in the form of a carriage and drawn by six mice. He takes one of the toads and puts it into this coach, and as soon as she sits down and they move along, she turns into a beautiful princess. Thus in order to get this most beautiful woman he cannot just seize her, as he does the carpet and the ring, but a special vehicle is needed. The lady toad is transformed when she sits in that carrot vehicle; only as it starts to carry her toward the king's palace, is she transformed.

In other versions, the beautiful girl exists from the very beginning. If you remember, in the Hessian version Dummling finds a beautiful girl spinning down in the earth, and it is only when she comes up that she appears as a frog. That is a very strange thing, for sometimes she is a toad or a frog in the earth and changes when she moves upward toward the human world, whereas in our story she becomes a human being when above the ground. In other versions, while down in the earth she is a beautiful human being and above, in the ordinary world, she is a frog, and only when Dummling jumps with her into a pond does she turn again into a human being. This is a relatively frequent variation: that under the earth she is already a human being but in the upper sphere appears as a frog or a toad or a dog. We therefore have to go into this symbolism more closely. We have already concluded from the steps and human construction in the earth that formerly the cult of the mother, or the relationship to the mother principle, must have been integrated into the realm of human awareness and later have regressed into the earth. Our story is concerned with bringing up something which was once realized in the human realm. The many parallels which tell us that a beautiful woman is sitting down in the earth waiting for her redemption confirm this hypothesis.

The anima—which means for a man the realm of fantasy and the way he relates to the unconscious—was once integrated in the field of consciousness and had reached a human level, but now, under unfavorable cultural circumstances, has been shut off and repressed into the unconscious. That explains why this beautiful princess is down in the cellar waiting for somebody to bring her up. It also explains why she is looked upon, and appears, as a frog. On the earth, at the king's court, a conscious attitude rules which sees the anima only as a frog. This means that in the conscious realm an attitude prevails which has a contemptuous "nothing but" outlook on the phenomenon of Eros, and in those circumstances the anima appears, in the eyes of these men at the king's court, to be a frog. We have a modern example of this in the Freudian theory in which the whole phenomenon of Eros is reduced to the biological sex functions. Whatever comes up is explained in the "nothing but" terms of rational theory. Freud had very little recognition of the feminine element and therefore always explained it as sex. From the Freudian standpoint, even a Gothic cathedral is only a morbid surrogate for unlived sex, as is proven by the phallic towers! Viewed from such a standpoint, the sphere of the anima cannot exist. However, it is not only the Freudian attitude that does this to the anima. A moral prejudice against Eros or a repression of the Eros principle for political or other reasons also may reduce the anima to a frog or a louse or whatever other form and level she may be repressed into. Then a man's anima becomes as undeveloped as the Eros function of a frog.

A frog, however, is not completely unrelated. It is possible to tame frogs, and you can make them take their food from you; they have a certain capacity for relatedness. Men who have a frog anima would behave in much the same way. So we understand why in the Hessian version an operation is needed to restore the human nature of the anima. In our main story it is the other way around. The anima appears below the earth as a toad, needing a carrot vehicle to bring her up and turn her into a human being.

In the Russian version of the frog-princess, Dummling has to introduce his frog-bride to the czar's court. He thinks that it will not be very agreeable when she turns up hopping along in the form of a frog, but she asks him to trust her and says that when he hears thunder he will know that she is putting on her wedding dress, and when he sees lightning he will know that she has finished dressing. Shivering with horror, he waits in the thunderstorm for his frog-bride to appear. Then she arrives as a most beautiful woman in a coach drawn by six dark horses, having transformed herself during this thunderstorm.

So this Russian Dummling has only to trust her and be ready

to stand by her even if she appears in a ridiculous and inhuman shape. In other versions there are mixtures of the frog-prince motif—namely, that she, like the famous frog-prince, asks to be accepted and to eat from his plate and be taken into his bed and be fully accepted in private life as a human being, with all the awkwardness that this imposes on the hero. Then she transforms herself into a human being. So we can say that she is generally redeemed by trust, acceptance, and love in different variations. But in our story she is not accepted by trust but is carried by the carrot vehicle. We have to go into the symbolism of the carrot. In the *Handwörterbuch des Deutschen Aberglaubens* (Dictionary of German Superstitions) you will find that the carrot has a phallic meaning. It is said in Baden that when you sow carrot seed you say, "I sow carrots, boys and girls, but if somebody steals some of them, may God grant that we have so many that we do not notice it." There it is quite clear that sowing carrot seed is like sowing girls and boys. In other countries they say, "Now I sow carrot seed *for* the boys and girls . . . "; then it continues in the same way. In the sowing of carrots there are a lot of other amusing allusions which all hinge on the fact that carrots seem to be food for very poor people, so when they are sown one must always be very generous and must say, "I sow these carrots, not only for myself but for my neighbors as well"; then one harvests a lot. Once, however, a man felt stingy and he said, "I sow carrots for myself and my wife." He got only two when he dug them up! Carrots contain a lot of water, probably the reason they are called *pissenlit* (piss-in-the-bed) in dialect.

From all this you see that the carrot, like most vegetables, has an erotic and especially a sexual meaning. You can say that the vehicle bringing up the anima is sex and sexual fantasy, which in a man's makeup is very often the way in which the world of Eros first wells up into his consciousness. It first is carried, as it were, by sexual fantasies.

Mice have in some ways also a similar meaning. In Greece they belong to the sun god Apollo, together with the rat, but they belong to the boreal or winter phase of Apollo, to the dark side of the sun principle. In Europe, mice belong to the devil, who is the ruler of mice and rats. He is mentioned in that way, for instance, in Goethe's *Faust:* "der Herr der Ratten und der Mäuse." In the *Handwörterbuch des deutschen Aberglaubens,* mice are looked on as being soul animals.[25] In our language it would mean that they very often represent the unconscious personality of a human being. For example, as I mentioned above, a bird leaving a body means that the soul is leaving the body. It can also happen that the soul leaves in the form of a mouse. In certain verses or rituals it is said that you should not hurt or insult mice because poor souls might dwell in them. In Chinese poetry there is a poem by one of the most famous Chinese poets, which to my mind beautifully describes what a rat means; mice have similar meanings.

> *Rat in my brain,*
> *I cannot sleep; day and night*
> *You gnaw out of me my life.*
> *I am slowly fading away,*
> *Oh, rat in my brain,*
> *Oh, my bad conscience.*
> *Will you never give me peace again?*

While the rat and the mouse do not necessarily stand for a bad conscience, the poet means any worrying thought that constantly and autonomously gnaws at and undermines one's attitude. You probably know those sleepless nights when you worry and every little thing becomes a mountain of difficulty; you cannot sleep and things go around in your head like a mill. It is really very similar to being disturbed by mice. Those damned creatures gnaw and nibble all night, and you bang on the wall, and for a time there is peace, and then they start again. If you have ever gone through that, you will recognize the analogy of the mouse and the worrying thought—a complex that gives you no peace. The mouse therefore represents an obsessive nocturnal thought or fantasy which bites you whenever you want to sleep. It very often also has an erotic quality, which you see in those cartoons in which women stand on tables with their skirts pulled up when a mouse runs about. Therefore, the Freudians generally interpret mice as sexual fantasies. This can be true when the obsessive gnawing thought *is* a sexual fantasy, but actually it can mean any kind of obsession which constantly gnaws at one's conscious mind. The carrot, meaning sex, and the mice, meaning nocturnal worries and autonomous fantasies, carry the anima figure up into the light. They appear to be the substructure of the anima.

When Dummling brings together the young toad and the vehicle, then the toad turns into a beautiful woman. This would mean, practically, that if a man has the patience and the courage to accept and bring to light his nocturnal sex fantasies, to look at what they carry and to let them continue, developing them and writing them down (which allows for further amplification), then his whole anima will come up into the light. If, when doodling, he says, "Now what am I doing here?" and develops the sex fantasy he has expressed in his drawing, then often the whole anima problem comes up and the anima is then much less inhuman and cold-blooded. The repressed feminine world comes with it, but the first triggering-off is very often a sexual fantasy or an obsession of some kind: the necessity to look at women's curves in the tram or looking at strip tease shows. If he lets such thoughts come up with whatever they bring with them, a man can in this way discover his anima, or rediscover her if he has repressed her for a while. If a man neglects relatedness, she at once regresses. And as soon as the anima becomes unconscious, then she also often becomes obsessional; she becomes a mouse again, so to speak, an intruding fantasy.

Even the third test does not convince the king and the two elder brothers, and here we come to a classic motif—that in fairy tales there are often three steps and then a finale. You will always read that the number three plays a big role in fairy tales, but when *I* count it is generally four. Here, for instance, there are three tests, it is true: the carpet, the ring, and the lady. But then there is the finale of jumping through the ring. Wherever you look you will see that this is a typical rhythm in fairy tales. There are three similar rhythms and then a final action. For instance, a girl loses her lover and has to find him again at the end of the world. She goes first to the sun, which shows her the way to the moon, which shows her the way to the night wind, and then she finds, as a fourth stage, her lover. Or the hero comes to three hermits or three giants, or he has to overcome three obstacles. The three are always clear units: 1, 2, 3, with a certain similar repetition, which is why the fourth is so often ignored, for the fourth is not just another additional number unit; it is not another thing of the same kind, but something completely different. It is as if one counted, one, two, three—bang! The one, two, and three lead up to the real *dénouement,* which is represented in the fourth and which is generally something static; there is no longer a leading-up, dynamic movement in it, but something comes to rest.

In number symbolism three is considered a masculine number (as all odd numbers are). It is the first, really, since the number one does not count as a number; it is the unique thing and therefore not yet a counting unit. So three is the first masculine odd number and represents the dynamism of the one. I can refer you to the number symbolism in Jung's paper "A Psychological Approach to the Dogma of the Trinity."[26] To put it very briefly, the three is generally connected with the flow of movement and thus with time, because there is no time without movement. There are the three Norns, which represent past, present, and future. Most of the gods of time are triadic. The three has always the symbolism of movement in it, because for movement you need two poles and the exchange of energy between them—for instance, the positive and negative electric pole and the current which equalizes the tension.

Often in mythology there is one figure accompanied by two acolytes (followers): Mithras and the Dadophores, Christ between the two thieves, and so on. Such triadic mythological formations stand for the oneness and its polarity, the one thing which unites, and the opposites as the two poles between which the uniting center appears. A certain difference has to be made between three things of the same kind, or a group of three where the one in the middle is really the whole thing and the two opposites are represented as a kind of illustration of what is within, of that wholeness. Or there is a dualism and a connecting third thing, but basically you never run off the main line if you keep in mind that the three has to do with movement and time, mostly an inexorable unilateral movement of life. That is why in fairy tales the story, the peripetia, is often divided into three phases, and then comes the fourth as a lysis or catastrophe. The fourth leads into a new dimension, which is not comparable to the three previous steps.

6

"THE THREE FEATHERS" COMPLETED

—— ❧❧❧❧❧❧ ——

Dummling now brings home his bride, who, sitting in her carrot carriage, has turned into a beautiful princess. But again when they arrive at the king's court the two elder brothers will not accept the solution and ask for a fourth and last test. A ring is suspended from the ceiling in the hall, and all three brides have to jump through that. The peasant women whom the two other brothers have brought jump but fall, breaking their arms and legs. But the youngest son's bride, probably on account of her past life as a frog or a toad, jumps through the ring with great elegance, so that now all protest is abandoned and the youngest son gets the crown and reigns for a long time in wisdom.

Earlier in the story we had the ring as a symbol of union. In its positive meaning, it stands for a consciously chosen obligation toward some divine power, that is, toward the Self; in its negative aspect it means fascination, being caught, being bound, with a negative connotation: for instance, being caught in one's complex or in one's emotions, being caught in a "vicious circle."

Here we have yet another motif—jumping through a ring. This comprises a double action since it means jumping high and at the same time being able to aim accurately at the center of the ring to get through it. In folklore there is mention of the old spring festivals in German countries, when, riding on horseback, the young men had to strike through the center of a ring with a spear. It was a spring fertility rite and at the same time an acrobatic test for the young men on their horses. There again is the motif of aiming at the center of the ring in a contest. This brings us closer to the meaning of aiming at, or through, the center of the ring. Though it seems rather remote, a connection can also be made with the Zen Buddhist art of archery, where the idea is to aim at the center, not in the extraverted way Westerners would do it, by physical skill and conscious concentration, but by a form of deep meditation by which the archer puts himself inwardly into his own center (what we would call the Self), from whence, naturally, he can hit the outer target. Thus, in their highest performances, with their eyes shut and without aiming, Zen Buddhist archers can effortlessly hit the target. The whole practice is meant as a technical help to find the way to dwell in one's own inner center without being diverted by thoughts and ambitions and ego impulses.

Now jumping through a burning ring is not practiced, as far as I can discover, except in the circus, where it is one of the most popular tricks. Tigers and other wild animals have to jump through burning rings. The more undomesticated the animal, the more exciting it is to see it jump through a ring, a motif to which I will return later.

Aiming accurately through the center of the ring is not so difficult to interpret. We could say that, although exteriorized in an outer symbolic action, it is the secret of finding the inner center of the personality and is absolutely parallel to what is attempted in Zen Buddhist archery. But there is a second difficulty. The person who jumps has to leave the earth—reality—and get at the center in a movement through midair. So the anima, the princess figure, when she goes through the center of the ring, is hovering in midair; it is specially emphasized that she could do this well. The peasant girls, however, were so heavy and awkward, the story says, that they could not do it without falling and breaking their legs, the gravitation of the earth being too strong for them.

This points to a very subtle problem in connection with the realization of the anima. Men who know nothing about psychology tend simply to project the anima onto a real woman, experiencing her entirely outside. But if through psychological introspection they realize that the attraction exerted upon them by the anima is not only an outer factor but is something they carry within themselves—an inner image of a feminine being which is the true ideal and the soul guide—then often, as a next problem, the ego raises a pseudo-conflict between the inner and the outer realms by saying, "I don't know if this dream figure is my anima inside or if it concerns the real woman outside. Shall I follow up an anima fascination in the external world, or shall I introject it and take it as purely symbolic?" When people use that phrase, there is a slight "nothing-but-purely-symbolic" undercurrent. With our strong disbelief in the reality of the psyche, people usually add something like, "Must I only realize it within? May I not have something outside and concrete as well?" There you see that consciousness, with its extraverted bias, gets caught in a false conflict between concrete outer and symbolic inner realization and in this way cuts the phenomenon of the anima artificially in two.

This only occurs if a man cannot lift his anima away from the earth, if she is not capable of jumping as the frog lady can, if she is like a peasant idiot. To get into this conflict indicates a lack of feeling-realization; it is a typical conflict, raised not by the feeling function but by thinking, which makes an artificial contrast between inside and outside, between ego and object. Actually the answer is that it is neither the outside nor the inside because it has to do with the reality of the psyche per se, and that is neither outside nor inside. It is both and neither. It is precisely *the anima* which has to be realized as a reality per se. If she, the anima, likes to come from outside, she has to be accepted there. If she likes to come from within, she has to be accepted there. The task is not to make any artificial and clumsy difference between the two realms. The anima is one phenomenon, the phenomenon of life. She represents the flow of life in a man's psyche. He has to follow up its tortuous ways, which move very specifically just between the two borders of inside and outside.

Another aspect of this pseudo-conflict is: "Must I think of my anima with spiritual devotion? For instance, pray to the Virgin instead of looking at a beautiful woman's legs and loving her sexually?" There is no such difference! The upper and lower are one and, like all contents of the unconscious, have a whole range of what we would call spiritual and instinctual manifestations. Basically in their archetypal appearance there is a oneness of those two factors, and only consciousness cuts these aspects apart. If a man has really learned to contact his anima, then this whole problem collapses, for then the anima will manifest immediately, and he will always remain concentrated on her reality and look away from such a pseudo-conflict which arises around her. To put it in very plain and simple words, he will try constantly to follow his feeling, his Eros side, without considering any other elements, and in that way walk through seemingly incompatible worlds on the razor's edge. Keeping to what Jung calls *the reality of the psyche* is an achievement like that of an acrobatic test, because our consciousness has the natural tendency always to be pulled into unilateral interpretations, always formulating a program or a recipe instead of simply keeping between the opposites with the flow of life. There is only one loyalty or constancy within all that: a loyalty to the inner reality of the anima, and this is beautifully expressed in the jumping through the ring, the anima in a midair position, accurately in the center and moving through it.

Another typical anima conflict raised by the unconscious to

force a man to differentiate his Eros is the marital triangle. When he gets into this conflict, he is liable to say, "If I cut off the other woman, I am betraying my own feeling for the sake of conventionality. If I run away from my wife and children with the woman on whom my anima projection has fallen, then I am behaving irresponsibly and following a mood that will collapse fairly soon, as one always knows. I cannot do both, and also I cannot prolong an impossible situation forever." (If the anima wants to impose herself upon a man's consciousness, she often brings about such a conflict.) His wife's animus will say, "You must make a decision!" And the girlfriend's animus goes up in the air and says, "I cannot just hang on like this!" Everyone and everything push him toward wrong decisions.

There again loyalty to the reality of the psyche gives the only possible solution, and generally the anima tends to maneuver a man into a situation which is *meant to be without issue.* Jung said that to be in a situation where there is no way out or to be in a conflict where there is no solution is the classical beginning of the process of individuation. It is *meant* to be a situation without solution: the unconscious wants the hopeless conflict in order to put ego consciousness up against the wall, so that the man has to realize that whatever he does is wrong, whichever way he decides will be wrong. This is meant to knock out the superiority of the ego, which always acts from the illusion that it has the responsibility of decision. Naturally, if a man says, "Oh well, then I shall just let everything go and make no decision, but just protract and wriggle out everywhere," the whole thing is equally wrong, for then naturally nothing happens. But if he is ethical enough to suffer to the core of his personality, then generally, because of the insolubility of the conscious situation, the Self manifests. In religious language you could say that the situation without issue is meant to force the man to rely on an act of God. In psychological language the situation without issue, which the anima arranges with great skill in a man's life, is meant to drive him into a condition in which he is capable of experiencing the Self, in which he will be inwardly open to an interference by the *tertium quod non datur* (the third, which is not given, that is, the unknown thing). In this way, as Jung said, the anima is the guide toward the realization of the Self, but sometimes in a very painful manner. When thinking of the anima as the soul guide, we are apt to think of Beatrice leading Dante up to Paradise, but we should not forget that he experienced that only after he had gone through Hell. Normally, the anima does not take a man by the hand and lead him right up to Paradise; she puts him first into a hot cauldron where he is nicely roasted for a while.

The anima in our story aims at the center, while the peasant women represent an undifferentiated, clumsy attitude which is glued too much to the idea of concrete reality, and therefore they fall short; they cannot stand the test, for they represent a too primitive and undifferentiated feeling attitude.

I would recommend in this connection Jung's talk given in 1939, "The Symbolic Life."[27] He says that we are now all caught in rationalism and that our rational outlook on life includes being reasonable and that this reasonableness excludes all symbolism. He goes on to show how much richer life is for people still embedded in the living symbolism of their religious forms. As Jung himself discovered, one can find the way back to some living symbolism— not to the lost symbolism, however, but to the still-living function that produces it. We get to it by attending to the unconscious and our dreams. By attending to one's dreams for a long time and by really taking them into consideration, the unconscious of modern man can rebuild a symbolic life. But that presupposes that you do not interpret your dreams purely intellectually and that you really incorporate them into your life. Then there will be a restoration of the symbolic life, no longer in the framework of a collective ritualistic form but more individually colored and shaped. This means no longer living merely with the reasonableness of the ego and its decisions but living with the ego embedded in a flow of psychic life which expresses itself in symbolic form and requires symbolic action.

We have to see what our own living psyche proposes as a symbolic life form in which we can live. Hence, Jung often insists on something which he did in his own life: when a dream symbol comes up in a dominating form, one should take the trouble to reproduce it in a picture, even if one does not know how to draw, or to cut it in stone, even if one is not a sculptor, and relate to it in some real manner. One should not go off from the analytical hour forgetting all about it, letting the ego organize the rest of the day; rather one should stay with the symbols of one's dreams the whole day and try to see where they want to enter the reality of one's life. This is what Jung means when he speaks of living the symbolic life.

The anima is the guide, or is even the essence of this realization of the symbolic life. A man who has not understood and assimilated his anima problem is not capable of living this inner rhythm; his conscious ego and his mind are not capable of telling him about it.

In the variation from another part of Germany that I mentioned last time, the frog is not transformed into the beautiful woman who appears at court; on the contrary, she appears in a frog shape in the upper world, whereas in the lower world she is a beautiful girl. There is also a final test; namely, the frog calls out: *Umschling mich* (embrace me) and *versenk dich* (immerse yourself). *Versenken* implies the action of lowering something into the water or into the earth. But it also means—especially when it is reflexive, *sich versenken*—to go into deep meditation. It is an expression used in mystical language. Naturally it depicts going down into your inner water or earth—or abyss—going down into your inner depths.

The frog anima makes this mysterious call, and Dummling understands it. He embraces the frog and jumps with her into the pool, and in that moment she transforms herself into a beautiful woman, and they come out together as a human couple. If we take that quite naively, we can say that Dummling has to follow her into *her* kingdom, accepting *her* way of life. She is a frog and jumps constantly into the water, swimming in it and enjoying it. If he embraces her and jumps with her into the water, then he accepts her frog life. So it can be said that the bridegroom follows the bride into *her* home instead of the other way around. Through his acceptance of her as a frog, she is transformed into a human being. Acceptance of the frog and the frog's life implies a jump into the inner world, sinking down into inner reality and there we come again to the same thing—that the anima's intention is to convert rational consciousness to acceptance of the symbolic life, sinking into it without any buts, criticisms, or rational objections but with a gesture of generous acceptance, saying, "In the name of God, whatever happens, I will jump into it and realize it." And that needs courage and naiveté. It means the sacrifice of the intellectual and rational attitude, which is difficult for women, but much more difficult for a man because it goes against his conscious tendencies, especially those of modern Western man.

When the anima becomes human, it is a meeting of the opposites: he goes toward her and so she comes up toward him. We always see that if the tension between the conscious situation and the too-low level of unconscious contents is too great, any gesture toward one side generally improves the other as well. Very often a man will dream, for instance, that his anima appears as a prostitute, or something like that, and he will say that she is too low down, that he cannot go as far as that; it is against his ethical principles. Generally, if someone overcomes such stiffened prejudices and makes a generous gesture toward the lower part of his personality and impulses, suddenly there is a change and the anima comes up onto a higher level. One should not, however, tell people that, for it would lessen the merit of the sacrifice which has to be made, courageously and absolutely without calculation. If one has such courage and truthfulness, then generally the miracle happens that this so-called low part of the personality, which has only been banished to that state by the haughtiness of the conscious attitude, comes up onto a human level.

There is a third version of our story which has a short continuation and a different form of the redemption of the frog lady, which also throws new light on what Jung means by the symbolic life. This is the Russian version of our story and is called "The Frog Daughter of the Czar."[28]

There was a czar and his wife. There were three sons, and they were like falcons, beautiful young men. One day the czar called them together and said, "My sons, my falcons, the time has come for you to find wives." He told them to take their silver bows and copper arrows and shoot them into foreign lands, and at whatever door the arrow fell, there each should find his bride. Two arrows fell into other czars' courts, and those men found relatively nice women. But Ivan Czarevitsch's arrow fell into a nearby swamp and there he found a frog with the arrow. He said, "Give me back my arrow." The frog replied, "I will return the arrow, but only on condition that you marry me." So Ivan Czarevitsch returned to the court and cried and related what had happened. The czar said, "Well, that's your bad luck, but you cannot get out of that; you must marry the frog." So the eldest son married a czar's daughter, the second son a prince's daughter, and the third son the green frog from the swamp.

In this story many things are different because there is a feminine influence at the court, so the king is not at all hostile to marriage with a frog; there is not such tension between male and female, or between acceptance and nonacceptance of frog life. But naturally Ivan is very unhappy. Then one day the czar wants to see which of his daughters-in-law can weave the most beautiful towel. Ivan goes home and cries, but the frog hops after him and tells him not to cry but to lie down and go to sleep and it will be all right. As soon as he is asleep she throws off her frog skin and goes out into the yard and calls and whistles. Her three maids and servants appear and weave the towels. When Ivan wakes up, they are given to him by his frog-wife, who has again assumed her frog skin. Ivan has never seen such towels in his life, and he takes them to the court and everybody is deeply impressed. Then there is another test as to who makes the best cake, and this is again made in the night while Ivan is asleep. The czar then tells his sons to come on a certain day with their wives to a dinner party. Ivan again goes home crying, but the frog-bride says he should not worry but should go on ahead. When he sees rain beginning to fall, he will know that his wife is washing. When the lightning comes, he will know that she is putting on her dress for the court. When he hears thunder, he will know that she is on the way. The dinner party begins and the two other wives are there beautifully dressed. Ivan is very nervous. A terrific thunderstorm begins. They all mock him and ask where his bride is. When the rain starts he says, "Now she is washing," and when there is lightning he says, "Now she is putting on her court dress." He does not believe it and is in despair, but when it thunders he says, "Now she is coming." And at that moment a beautiful coach with six horses arrives, and out of it steps a most beautiful girl—so beautiful that everyone becomes quite silent and shy.

At the dinner table the other two daughters-in-law notice something very strange, for the beautiful girl puts a part of her food into her sleeves. The other two brides think it very odd but that it may be good manners, and they do the same thing. When the dinner is over there is music and dancing. The former frog-girl dances with Ivan Czarevitsch and is so light and dances so beautifully that she hardly seems to touch the floor. As she dances she waves her right arm and out of it falls a bit of the food, which is transformed into a garden with a pillar in it. Around this a tomcat circles, then climbs up it and sings folk songs. When it comes down it tells fairy tales. The girl goes on dancing and makes a gesture with her left hand, and there appears a beautiful park with a little river in it and on the river, swans. Everybody is as astonished at the miracle as if they were little children. The other sisters begin to dance, but when they throw out their right arm, a bone comes out and hits the czar on the forehead, and when they fling out the left arm, water shoots into his eyes.

Ivan looks in amazement at his wife and wonders how out of a green frog there could emerge such a beautiful girl. He goes into the room where she slept and sees the frog skin lying there. He picks it up and throws it into the fire. Then he goes back to the court and they go on amusing themselves till morning, when Ivan goes home with his wife.

When they get home his wife goes to her room and cannot find her frog skin. At last she calls out and asks Ivan if he has seen her dress. "I burnt it," says Ivan. "Oh, Ivan," she says, "what have you done? If you had not touched it, I would have been yours forever. But now we must separate—perhaps forever!" She cries and cries, and then says, "Good-bye! Seek me in the Thirtieth Czar's Kingdom, in the Thirtieth Strange Kingdom, where there is the Baba Yaga, the great witch, and her bones." And she claps her hands and changes into a cuckoo and flies out of the window.

Ivan grieves bitterly. Then he takes his silver bow and fills a sack with bread, hangs bottles over his shoulder, and goes on his long quest. He walks for many years.

He meets an old man who gives him a ball of thread and tells him he should follow it to the Baba Yaga. Then he spares the life of a bear, a fish, and a bird. He gets into all sorts of difficulties, but the fish and falcon and bear help him, and finally, at the end of the world in the Thirtieth Kingdom, he comes to an island on which there is a forest and in it a glass palace. He goes into the palace and opens an iron door, but nobody is inside; then he opens a silver door, but there is nobody in the room, so he opens a third door made of gold, and behind this door sits his wife combing flax. She looks so woebegone and careworn that she is dreadful to look at. But when she sees Ivan she falls on his neck and says, "Oh my beloved, how I have longed for you. You have arrived just in time. Had you come out just a little later, you might perhaps never have seen me again." And she cries for joy. Although Ivan does not know whether he is in this world or the next, they embrace and kiss. Then she changes herself into a cuckoo, takes Ivan under her wing, and flies back. When they arrive home she changes again into human form and says, "It was my father who had cursed me and had given me to a dragon to serve for three years, but now I have paid the penalty." So they came home and lived happily together and praised God, who had helped them.

In our Russian version, instead of jumping through the ring, the anima figure performs this fantastic magic with the food which she puts into her sleeve and transforms into the garden with the tomcat who sings songs and tells fairy tales and the paradise which she creates with her left hand. In this way you see even more clearly that the anima creates the symbolic life, for she transforms ordinary food for the body into spiritual food through creating art and mythologial tales; she restores paradise, a kind of archetypal world of fantasy. The tomcat represents a nature spirit which is the creator of folk songs and fairy tales. It also shows the close connection of the anima with man's capacity for artistic work and with the fantasy world. A man who represses his anima generally represses his creative imagination.

Dancing and creating a kind of *fata morgana,* a fantasy world, is a similar motif to jumping through the ring. It is still another aspect of creating the symbolic life, which one lives by following up one's dreams and day fantasies and the impulses which come up from the unconscious, for fantasy gives life a glow and a color which the too-rational outlook destroys. *Fantasy* is not just whimsical ego-nonsense but comes really from the depths; it constellates symbolic situations which give life a deeper meaning and a deeper realization. Here again, the two other figures take this too concretely. Just as the peasant women could not jump through the ring but broke their legs, here they put food in their sleeves for wrong motives, for ambition, and accordingly fall short.

But then there is something else: Ivan makes a mistake by burning his wife's frog skin. This is a most widespread motif to be found in completely different connections in many other fairy tales. The anima first appears in an animal skin, either as a fish or a mermaid, or, most frequently, as a bird, and then she turns into a human being. Generally her lover keeps her former animal skin or bird garment in a drawer. The woman has children and everything seems to be all right, but unfortunately either the husband insults his wife one day, calling her a mermaid or a goose or whatever she was before, and she rushes to her old garment, puts it on again, and disappears, and either he has to go on a long quest to find her again, or she disappears forever and he dies. In such stories one feels that it would have been better if the man burnt the skin, because if she finds it, she disappears in it. But here it is just the opposite. He burns the skin, which would seem to be all right, and it is wrong again! In other fairy tales—for instance, the Grimms' tale called "Hans the Hedgehog," the animal skin is also burnt. A prince has been cursed and turned into a hedgehog and the bride's servants burn the hedgehog skin, and that frees him and he gives thanks for being redeemed. So the burning of the animal skin is not in itself necessarily destructive; it depends on the context.

We never learn in our story why the burning of the skin causes the wife to fly away. We can imagine that because of her father's curse she must still go into the night and atone for her sins, and since that is interrupted, the punishment becomes more definite. But this is speculation; the story gives no explanation. The fairy tales in which the animal skin is successfully burned belong to the many rituals of transformation by fire. In most mythological accounts, fire has a purifying and transforming quality and is therefore used in many religious rituals. In alchemy fire is used—as some texts say, literally—to "burn away all superfluities," so that only the indestructible nucleus remains. Consequently, the alchemists burn most of their substances first, destroying what can be destroyed. That which resisted fire was looked on as a symbol of immortality—the solid kernel which survives destruction. Fire is therefore the great transformer. In certain Gnostic texts fire is also called the great judge because it judges, so to speak, what is worthy of survival and what should be destroyed. In its psychological meaning, where it generally stands for the heat of emotional reactions and affects, all that applies too. Without the fire of emotion no development takes place and no higher consciousness can be reached, which is why God says, "Because thou art lukewarm, and neither cold nor hot, I will spew thee out of my mouth" (Rev. 3:16). If someone in analysis is dispassionate about it and does not suffer—if there is neither the fire of despair nor hatred nor conflict nor fury nor annoyance nor anything of that kind—one can be pretty sure that not much will be constellated and it will be a "blah-blah" analysis forever. So the fire, even if it is a destructive sort of fire—conflicts, hatred, jealousy, or any other affect—speeds up the maturing process and really is a "judge" and clarifies things.

People who have fire run into trouble, but at least they try something, they fall into despair. The more fire there is, the more there is danger of the destructive effects of emotional outbursts, of all sorts of mischief and devilry, but at the same time this is what keeps the process going. If the fire is extinct, everything is lost. That is why the alchemists always said one must never let one's fire go out. The lazy worker who lets his fire go out is just lost. He is the person who only nibbles at analytical treatment but never goes into it wholeheartedly. He has no fire, and therefore nothing happens. So the fire is really the great judge and determines the difference between the corruptible and the incorruptible, between what is relevant and what is irrelevant, and therefore in all magical and religious rituals fire has a sacred and transforming quality. In many myths, however, fire is the great destroyer; sometimes a myth depicts the destruction of the world by fire. Those dreams in which whole towns are burned down or your own house is burned down as a rule indicate an already existing affect that has become completely out of control. Whenever an emotion overruns one's self-control, then comes the motif of the destructive fire. Have you ever, in a state of affect, done horrible, irremediable things? Haven't you ever written a letter that you would give anything not to have written? Or said something because of which you could bite out your tongue? Perhaps you have done destructive things through emotion—something you cannot mend, something ruined forever, a relationship with another human being destroyed. Last but not least are the declarations of war—often made in a state of affect—and then the destruction *does* lead to a world conflagration. Destructive affect, as one knows from mass phenomena, is exceedingly infectious. Someone who drops the reins and gives way to destructive emotion can generally pull in many other people, and then there occur those terrific mass outbursts in which people are lynched or shot—all due to a sudden fire of affect getting loose.

There you see, literally, the fearful destructiveness of the fiery emotion; you find it also in psychotic constellations, where underneath a rigid surface terrific emotions are piled up. An outburst is often represented as a huge conflagration in which everything is destroyed; then the individual gets into a state of excitement, becoming so dangerous to himself or others that he has to be interned.

The burning of the frog skin indicates the destructive effect of fire, but we must also take into consideration the fact that the frog is a cold-blooded animal and a water creature—water being the opposite of fire—and therefore she is a creature that dwells in moisture. That probably is another reason why application of fire to her skin is specifically destructive here. It takes away the princess's water quality. What does it mean psychologically if a man applies destructive fire to his "moist," creative anima? We have seen that the anima in this context—and also in practical life—represents the gift of poetic fantasy, the ability to create the symbolic forms of life. If, therefore, the hero applies fire to her skin, that would mean a too analytical, too impulsive, too passionate concern with the creative fantasy. By grabbing their own fantasies and pulling them too eagerly into the light of consciousness and by interpreting them at once with too much intensity, many people destroy their secret inner life.

Creativity sometimes needs the protection of darkness, of being ignored. That is very obvious in the natural tendency many artists and writers have not to show their paintings or writings before they are finished. Until then they cannot stand even positive reactions. The passionate reactions of people to a painting, the exclamation, "Oh, this is wonderful!," may, even if meant in a positive way, entirely destroy the chiaroscuro, the mystical hidden weaving of fantasy which the artist needs. Only when he has finished his product can he expose it to the light of consciousness, and to the emotional reactions of others. Thus if you notice an unconscious fantasy coming up within you, you would be wise not to interpret it at once. Do not say that you know what it is and force it into consciousness. Just let it live with you, leaving it in the half-dark, carry it with you and watch where it is going or what it is driving at. Much later you will look back and wonder what you were doing all that time, that you were nursing a strange fantasy which then led to some unexpected goal. For instance, if you do some painting and have the idea that you could add this and that, then don't think, "I know what that means!" If you do, then push the thought away and just give yourself to it more and more so that the whole web of symbols expands in all its ramifications before you jump at its essential meaning.

Hence, if people do active imagination in analysis, I generally only listen to it and only at the special request of the analysand, or if the fantasies are too overflowing and therefore need cutting down, or if they have already found a certain end, can one analyze them like a dream. It is much better not to analyze them while they are going on, for then the author of the fantasy becomes self-conscious and knows what it could be about, which inhibits further working of the fantasy.

If an unconscious fantasy or another content is especially fiery, heavily laden with affect, it will push through to consciousness, no matter what. But there are certain fantasies that are more froglike; that is, they come up in the daytime as a kind of playful thought; in an idle moment you light a cigarette, and a strange fantasy comes, but without much energetic load. If you jump in a fiery way onto such thoughts, you destroy them. These, like the little creatures—the dwarfs, and such creatures—you must not look at; just let them be around you and do not disturb their secret work. Our frog-woman belongs more to this latter category of creatures because we see from her tomcat that her spirit sings folk songs and tells fairy tales, and that is an artistic, playful spirit which could be destroyed by being taken too seriously, with too much affect. That is probably why Ivan made such a big mistake in burning the frog skin. By that he delayed the definite redemption of his anima.

That he can find her again at the end of the world is something which occurs in many fairy tales. A man meets his destined bride and by some mistake loses her again and then has to go on an endless journey into the underworld and through seven heavens to find her again. This double rhythm corresponds to what one could technically call the first apparent blossoming at the beginning of an analysis. It happens often to people who have for a long while stiffened in a neurotic conscious attitude and have therefore lost contact with the flow of life and have lost hope of getting out of their neurotic rut. When they come into analysis and receive the warm concern of another human being and through dreams a sudden contact with irrational possibilities, or if a prospective dream shows that in spite of the apparently hopeless aspect of life in consciousness there is an irrational positive possibility in the unconscious, then often, after the first hours of analysis, there comes a remarkable blossoming; the symptoms disappear and the individual experiences a miraculous healing. Never fall for that! In only five percent of the cases does it last. In all other cases, after a while the whole misery flows in again and the symptoms return. Such an initial blossoming usually occurs when the faulty conscious neurotic attitude is far away from the unconscious life tendencies, so that it is impossible to link the two sides. You first link them and things seem all right, but then both opposites stiffen again and everything falls back. Healing has really taken place only when there is a constant state of relationship between consciousness and the unconscious, not when through a relationship a spark flies over, but only when a condition of continual relationship with the other side has been established. To build that up generally takes a long time, and only then can you say that a healing cure is really solidified and safe from relapses. This first blossoming, however, is an archetypal event.

I have often asked myself why the unconscious or nature—or whatever we want to call it—plays such a cruel trick on people by first curing them and then dropping them again. Why should one hang a good sausage under a dog's nose and then take it away? That's not nice. But I have seen that there is a deep meaning and probably a final intention in this. If some people had not had a brief experience and glimpse of how it could be when things are right, they would never hold on through the miseries of the analytical process. It is only the remembrance of that glimpse of paradise that makes them continue on the dark journey. This is probably one reason why sometimes, at the beginning of analysis, the unconscious offers the marvelous possibility of cure and of the right kind of life and of happiness, and then takes it away; it is as if it were to say: "That is what you will get later, but you first have to realize this and this and this, and much more, before you can get there." I found that out practically when people who had experienced an early blossoming said, "Well, after all, I was without symptoms at such and such a time, so it should be possible, shouldn't it?" Yes, it should be possible. And that gives them the courage to hold on in a desperate situation. In our fairy tale, if Ivan had not seen his bride in her beautiful state and had not had that relationship with her, he would certainly not have walked to the Thirtieth Czar's Kingdom at the end of the world.

In this story there is another interesting motif. The frog-lady has been cursed by her father for some sin she has committed. We are not even sure that it was a sin—it was probably only a sin in the eyes of her father—but she has done something which annoyed him and has been cursed and has to live in the form of a frog and be in the hands of a dragon, and Ivan must rescue her from there.

That is complicated, if we think about it psychologically, because in our main story, "The Three Feathers," we had assumed that the anima was in the low form of a toad because consciousness had no relationship to the feminine side. In the conscious situation there was only a king and his three sons and no feminine principle, so that the whole feminine world was repressed and existed in a degenerate form. Now here the balance of the story is completely different because at the beginning the czar has a wife; there is a mother principle—the feminine principle is not lacking in the conscious setup—and accordingly we cannot speak simply of the repression of the anima. There is another difficulty: the frog-lady has annoyed her father, about whom we do not know much, and he has cursed her and brought her into this low condition. The accompanying diagram makes it clearer. At the top there are five people instead of four, so it is a completely different setup. You could say that that is a naturally balanced family; there is a little bit more of the male than of the female, but nothing vital is lacking. Below the threshold of consciousness are the frog-lady and her father.

Now the father below, who is only mentioned at the end of our story, puts a negative curse on his daughter which takes her away from consciousness into the depths of the unconscious. So

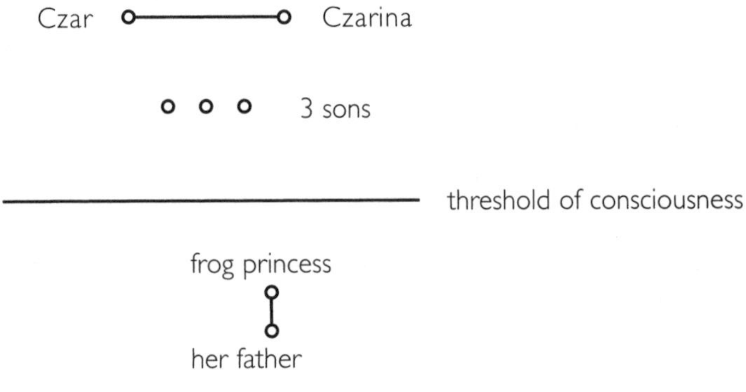

Czar o————o Czarina

o o o   3 sons

———————————————— threshold of consciousness

frog princess
o
o
her father

really her father deflects her path and prevents her coming up and being integrated, which would be the normal process in life. Why the father of the frog-lady is so bad-tempered we do not know, but he certainly seems not to want his daughter to marry on the conscious level. The only thing we can assume is that he has some reason against her becoming conscious. He wants to keep her to himself, perhaps, as fathers often do, but we do not know, and it is no good speculating about such family troubles in the unconscious. (Family troubles in the unconscious are something terrific, if you reflect.) Translated into psychological language, it means that one unconscious archetypal complex fights another archetypal complex within the unconscious. In my experience, such a conflict is generally a ricochet effect of some disturbance between the two worlds of the conscious and unconscious sphere. I assume, but I could give you other examples where it becomes clear, that the father below has a conflict-tension with the upper czar. Those two fathers fight, and instead of attacking the czar, the lower father takes his daughter away.

Who is this father of the frog-princess? Who is the anima's father? In many European stories in which there is a Christian influence, the father of the anima is called the devil. In European countries with less Christian influence, the father of the anima is characterized as the older image of God. For instance, in Germanic countries the anima's father appears as an old man with a Wotanic character, in Jewish legends he is an old desert god or a demon; in Islamic fairy tales the fathers of the anima are great jinns, which means pagan demons of the pre-Islamic time. In general, therefore, the frog-princess's father would represent an older image of God which is in contrast to, and repressed by, the new dominant God-image. The new ruling dominant of consciousness usually superimposes itself on an older image of the same kind, and often there is still a secret tension between these two factors. That is what makes the anima diverge in this way.

This is important in practical life also; for example, we often see that a man's anima is an old-fashioned being. She is frequently bound to the historical past, and this explains why men who in conscious life are courageous innovators, inclined toward change and reform, become sentimentally conservative as soon as they fall into an anima mood. They can be amazingly sentimental; for example, a thoroughly ruthless businessman who thinks nothing of ruining people will sing childhood songs under the Christmas tree, as if he couldn't hurt a fly. His anima has remained in the traditional world of childhood. You can see the same thing in the area of Eros—for instance, the belief in institutions held by some men. This too is an anima effect. With such beliefs men are strongly bound to the past. Women, who are known to be more conservative in their conscious lives (which accounts for the statement that they would still stir the soup with a stick if men had not invented a spoon), often have an animus with an eye to the future and a talent for effecting changes. This is often seen in women's interest in new movements. In ancient Greece, the Dionysian cult was for the most part picked up first by women and carried out by them. Then again, the early Christian communities were mainly carried by the enthusiasm of women, not men.

When the old God-image binds the anima to the past, then naturally a rift opens up between the new conscious attitude and the older layer, where the anima comes from. So there is a germ of truth in the contention that the telling of fairy tales belongs to the paganism of the past, as the Grimm Brothers said. According to the Russian story, the frog-princess is the fairy tale teller, and she cannot quite come up to the realm of the ruling czar. The real conflict is between the two father figures. This is something one often meets with if there is a conflict in the unconscious; that is, one unconscious content hits some other content in the unconscious, and instead of hitting back, the other content hits still another one, and so there is an indirect effect. This is illustrated by the famous story of the lady who scolds the cook, who shouts at the kitchen maid, who kicks the dog, who bites the cat—and so on. The conflict is passed on and then comes up in a completely different realm, and you do not know where the real conflict lies. This is why one must always look at the parallels and at the whole context to find out the deeper connections. They sometimes lead into unfathomable depths, such as here, where it is a question of the image of God. In our main German story it is a question of wrenching the anima away from the depths of the earth—the womb of Mother Nature—while in the Russian story she also has to be liberated from a dark negative father god. But we will stop here and continue discussing the methods of interpretation.

7

SHADOW, ANIMA, AND ANIMUS IN FAIRY TALES

Though nearly all fairy tales ultimately circle around the symbol of the Self or are "ordered" by it, we also find in many stories motifs which remind us of Jung's concepts of the shadow, animus, and anima. In this chapter I will give the interpretation of an example of each of these motifs. But we must again realize that we are dealing with the objective, impersonal substructure of the human psyche and not with its personal individual aspects.

The figure of the shadow in itself belongs partly to the personal unconscious and partly to the collective unconscious. In fairy tales only the collective aspect can occur—the shadow of the hero, for instance. This figure appears as a shadow-hero, more primitive and more instinctive than the hero but not necessarily morally inferior. In some fairy tales, the hero (or heroine) has no shadow companion but displays in himself both positive and negative traits, sometimes demonic traits. We must ask, therefore, in what psychological circumstances does the hero-image split into a light figure and a shadow companion. A division of this sort often occurs in dreams in which an unknown figure appears for the first time, and the split indicates that the approaching content is only partially acceptable to consciousness. Becoming conscious of something presupposes a choice on the part of the ego. Generally only one aspect of the unconscious content can be realized at one time, the other aspects being rejected. The shadow of the hero is therefore that aspect of the archetype which has been rejected by collective consciousness.

Even though the shadow figure in fairy tales is archetypal, from its characteristic behavior we can learn a great deal about the assimilation of the shadow in the personal realm. In order to illustrate this, I shall take the Norwegian story "Prince Ring."[29] Although collective, this tale provides analogies to the individual problem of the integration of the shadow and shows what features of this process are typical and general.

Prince Ring

Ring, the son of a king, while out hunting one day was captivated by the sight of a fleet hind with a golden ring around her horns. Wildly pursuing her, he became separated from his companions and rode into a thick fog in which he lost sight of the hind. Slowly he made his way out of the wood and came to a beach where he found a woman hunched over a barrel. Approaching, he saw the golden ring lying in the barrel, and the woman, guessing his desire, suggested that he take the ring. As he reached into the barrel, he found that it had a deceptive bottom, so that the deeper he reached, the farther away the ring appeared to be. When he himself was halfway down, the woman flipped him in, made the cover secure, and rolled the barrel into the surf. The outgoing tide bore him away.

After a very long time the barrel was washed ashore, and Ring climbed out on a strange island. Before he had time to get his bearings, a huge giant had picked him up out of curiosity and carefully carried him home as company for his giant wife. These old giants were very affable and deferred to the king's son's every wish. The giant freely showed the youth his treasures, only forbidding him to enter his kitchen. Prince Ring felt an immense curiosity to know what was in the kitchen and twice was on the verge of entering but stopped himself. The third time he had the courage to look, and a dog called out several times, "Choose me, Prince Ring! Choose me!"

After some time the giants, knowing that they would soon die, told Ring that they were about to depart this life and offered to give him anything he chose. Ring recalled the dog's urgent plea and asked for what was in the kitchen. The giant was not well pleased but consented. The dog—called Snati-Snati—leaped up wildly in his joy at being with Ring, and the prince was a little afraid.

They journeyed to a kingdom on the mainland, and Snati-Snati told Ring to ask the king for a small room where he might spend the winter as a guest of the palace. The king welcomed him, but the brow of Rauder, his minister, grew dark with jealousy. Rauder pressed the king to hold a contest wherein he and the new guest would cut down trees to see who could make the biggest clearing in the forest in a single day. Snati-Snati urged Ring to get two axes, and they both began the task. By evening Snati-Snati had felled half again as many trees as the minister. Then, at Rauder's urging, the king ordered Ring to kill two wild bulls in the forest and return with their skins and horns. In the encounter Snati-Snati came to the aid of Ring, who had been knocked down, and ferociously killed the bulls. He stripped them of their skins and horns, which he brought to the castle, and Ring was greatly lauded for the deed. Next Ring had to recover the three most precious objects, objects now in the possession of a family of giants in a nearby mountain: a golden suit of clothes, a golden chessboard, and shining gold itself. If he could retrieve these, he might then marry the king's daughter.

Carrying a big sack of salt, man and dog—Ring holding onto the tail of the dog—laboriously climbed the steep mountain and with difficulty arrived at the top. They found a cave, and looking through the opening, they discerned four giants sleeping around a fire, over which boiled a pot of groats. Swiftly they dumped the salt into the pot. When the giants

awoke, they fell greedily on their meal, but after a few mouth-
fuls the giant-mother, who was terrible to look at, roared with
thirst and begged her daughter to fetch water. The daughter
agreed only on condition that she should have the shining gold.
After a furious scene, the giant-mother relinquished it to her.
When the daughter did not return, the old woman sent her
son, who first wangled from her the golden clothes and then
was drowned in the same manner. The ruse also worked with
the husband, who took with him the golden chessboard, the
only difference being that the old man rose again as a ghost
and had to be finally beaten down. The prince and Snati-Snati
then faced the terrible witch-giantess and, as Snati-Snati
pointed out, no weapon could penetrate her; she could only
be killed with the cooked groats and a red-hot iron. When the
witch saw the dog in the entrance to the cave, she croaked,
"Oh, it is you and Prince Ring who have killed my family!"
They joined in a desperate struggle, and she was brought to
her death. After burning the corpses, Ring and Snati-Snati returned with the treasures, and Prince Ring became engaged to
the king's daughter.

On the evening before the marriage the dog begged to
exchange places with Ring, with the result that he slept in
Ring's bed and Ring slept on the floor. During the night,
Rauder, intent on murdering Ring, stealthily entered the room
with a drawn sword and approached the bed, but as he raised
his arm, Snati-Snati leaped up and bit off his right hand. In
the morning, before the king, Rauder accused Ring of having
wantonly attacked him. Then Ring produced the severed hand
still gripping the sword, and the king thereupon had his minister hanged.

Ring married the princess, and on the wedding night
Snati-Snati was allowed to lie at the foot of the bed. In the
night he regained his true form, that of a king's son also named
Ring. His stepmother had changed him into a dog, and he
could only be redeemed by sleeping at the foot of the bed of a

king's son. The hind with the golden ring, the woman on the beach, and the formidable witch-giantess were in reality different guises of his stepmother, who wished at any price to prevent his redemption.

This tale opens with the image of a prince hunting. Many fairy tales—more than half, in fact—have to do with members of a royal family; in the others, the heroes are ordinary people such as poor peasants, millers, deserters, and so on. But in our story the main figure represents a future king; that is, a still unconscious element which is capable of becoming a new collective dominant and which will make possible a deeper understanding of the Self.

The prince chases a deer that has a golden ring between its horns. The Greek parallel to this is the Kerynitic hind with golden antlers, sacred to Artemis, which Hercules pursued for a year but was not allowed to kill.[30] In one version of the myth, he finally finds her in the Hesperides under the apple trees, which bestow eternal youth. Artemis, the famous huntress, is often transformed into a deer; in other words, the hunter and the hunted are secretly identical.

The hind frequently shows the way or finds the most advantageous point for the crossing of a river. On the other hand, she sometimes lures the hero to disaster or even to death by leading him over a precipice or into the sea or a swamp. She can also nurture an orphan or an abandoned child. The stag often carries a ring or a precious cross between his horns, or he may have golden horns. (By depicting a hind with horns our fairy tale indicates that the deer is feminine—an anima motif—and at the same time assigns horns to her as a masculine trait, thereby implying that this is a hermaphroditic being which unites the elements of the anima and the shadow.) A medieval tradition tells that when the stag feels old, he first eats a snake and then swallows enough water to drown it; at the same time, however, the snake poisons him, and the stag must shed his antlers to rid himself of the poison. Once the poison is gone, he may grow new horns. "Therefore," a Father of the Church declares, "the stag knows the secret of self-renewal; he sheds his antlers, and thus should we learn to shed our pride." The shedding of the antlers is probably the natural basis of all of the mythological transformation attributes of the deer. In medieval medicine, the bone in the heart of the deer was thought to be beneficial for heart trouble.

To sum up, the deer symbolizes an unconscious factor which shows the way that leads to a crucial event, either toward rejuvenation (that is, a change in the personality or in the beloved) or into the Beyond (i.e., the Hesperides)—or even to death. Furthermore, the deer is a bearer of light and of mandala symbols (the circle and the cross). Like Mercurius or Hermes, the deer seems to be a typical psychopomp—a guide into the unconscious. Functioning as a bridge to the deeper regions of the psyche, it is a content of the unconscious which attracts consciousness and leads it to new knowledge and new discoveries. As the instinctive wisdom that resides in man's nature, the deer exerts a strong fascination and represents that unknown psychic factor which endows all images with meaning. Its death aspect arises when consciousness has a negative attitude toward it; such an attitude forces the unconscious into a destructive role.

In our tale the deer bears a ring on its horns, and the king's son is called Ring, thereby revealing that the stag carries an essential component of the prince's own nature—namely, his undomesticated, instinctive side. Together they are the complementary sides of that psychic entity of which the prince is the anthropomorphic aspect. At first he is an aimless hunter, having not yet discovered his individual forms of realization. Incomplete, he represents merely the possibility of becoming conscious, and therefore he has to find his own opposite in the same way that the stag in the allegory swallows and integrates its opposite in the form of the snake (in some versions, a toad). It is therefore understandable that the deer possesses the secret of the prince's renewal and completion—the golden ring, which is a symbol of wholeness.

The prince goes hunting in the woods—that is, in the unconscious realm—and gets lost in a fog, so that vision is dim and all boundaries are wrapped in mist. Losing his comrades means isolation and the loneliness typical of the journey into the unconscious. The center of interest has shifted from the outer world to the inner, but the inner world is still completely unintelligible. At this stage, the unconscious seems senseless and bewildering.

The deer leads the prince to a beach where an evil woman sits hunched over a barrel. The object of fascination, the ring, has apparently been cast into the barrel by the hind. The ring is a symbol of the Self, especially as a factor that creates relatedness; it means the completion of the inner essential being, and this is what the prince is seeking. Pursuing the golden ring and led by the attraction of the deer, the prince falls into the hands of a witch, who, as we learn later, is Snati-Snati's stepmother. In masculine psychology the stepmother is a symbol of the unconscious in its destructive role—of its disturbing and devouring character.

He plunges into the cask after the ring. The stepmother swiftly shuts the cask and rolls it into the sea, a seeming misfortune which turns out to be fortunate because he is thrown onto an island where he finds Snati-Snati, his magic double and helpful companion. Thus the stepmother has an equivocal character: with one hand she destroys and with the other she leads to fulfillment. Being the frightful mother, she represents a natural resistance that blocks the development of higher consciousness, a resistance that calls forth the hero's best qualities. In other words, by persecuting him, she helps him. As the king's second wife, the stepmother is, in a way, a false wife, and since she belongs to the old system that the

king represents, she must stand for the dull, leaden unconsciousness which accompanies ancestral social institutions and which
works against the tendency to develop a new state of consciousness.
This stubbornly negative unconsciousness has the shadow of the
prince in thrall.

When the hero is set adrift in the cask, the cask is the vessel
that sustains him upon the waters, and in this aspect it is motherly
and protective; moreover, it allows the water currents to bear him
to the intended place. Looked at negatively, however, it denotes a
regression into the womb and is a prison that isolates him. In this
image the confusion and feeling of being lost and unable to find a
way out suggested by the motif of the fog are intensified. On the
plane of psychological reality this can be interpreted as a state of
possession by an archetype—in this case, a state of possession by
the mother. One can say that Prince Ring is now under the spell
of a negative mother-image which seeks to cut him off from life
and to swallow him.

The cask corresponds to the whale in the story of Jonah, and
the prince's traveling in it is a typical night-sea journey; it is, in
other words, a state of transition in which the hero is enclosed in
the mother-image as in a vessel. But the cask not only imprisons
the hero; it also prevents him from being drowned. This can be
compared to a neurosis, which tends to isolate the individual and
in that way to protect him. The condition of neurotic loneliness is
positive when it protects the growth of a new possibility of life. It
can be a stage of incubation which aims at the inner completion of
a more real and more definitely shaped conscious personality. This
is the meaning of the cask for Prince Ring.

Like the cask, the island is another symbol of isolation. It is
generally a magic realm inhabited by otherworldly figures, and on
this island there are giants. Islands often harbor projections of the
unconscious psychic sphere; for instance, there are islands of the

dead, and in *The Odyssey* the imprisoning nymph Calypso, the "veiled one," and the sorceress Circe both live on islands, and in a way both are goddesses of death. In our story the island is not the hero's goal but another stage in the transition. In the sea of the unconscious the island represents a split-off portion of the conscious psyche (as we know, beneath the sea, islands are usually connected with the mainland), and here the island represents an autonomous complex, quite apart from the ego, with a kind of intelligence of its own. Magnetic and evasive, it is a little island of consciousness, and its effect can be subtle and insidious.

Undeveloped people frequently have incongruous and quite separate complexes that almost jostle one another: for instance, incompatible Christian and pagan concepts which are not recognized as being mutually contradictory. The complex builds up its own field of "consciousness" apart from the original field, where the old viewpoint still prevails, and it is as if each is an independent island of consciousness with its own harbors and traffic.

On this island dwell giants. Giants are characterized only by their size and have a close relation to natural phenomena; in folk belief, for example, thunder is thought to be giants bowling or to be the resounding blows of storm-giants hammering; erratic stone formations are composed of stones tossed by giants in play, and fog appears when the giantesses hang up their washing. There are different families of giants: storm-giants, earth-giants, and so on. Mythologically, giants often appear as the "older people" in creation, a race that has died out: "There were giants in the earth in those days" (Gen. 6:4). In some cosmogonies they are featured as the forerunners of human beings who did not make the grade; for instance, in the *Edda,* Sutr, the giant, is portrayed with a sword which separates the opposite poles, fire and ice, and the *Edda* goes on to tell of the creation of the giant Ymir from the mixture of these opposites. (Then Ymir was butchered, and dwarfs emerged as worms from his entrails.) The Greek giants are the Titans who rebelled against Zeus and were slain by his lightning. In the Orphic tradition men issued from the smoke of their burned flesh. Or the giants became drunk with hubris and were therefore destroyed by the gods; and then men inherited their earth. Giants, therefore, are a supernatural race, older and only half human. They represent emotional factors of crude force, factors which have not yet emerged into the realm of human consciousness. Giants possess enormous strength and are renowned for their stupidity. They are easy to deceive and a prey to their own affects, and therefore helpless for all their might. The powerful emotional impulses they stand for are still rooted in archetypal subsoil, and when one falls victim to such boundless impulses, one is wild, overpowered, beside oneself, berserk—and one is as stupid as a giant; one may display gigantic strength and afterward collapse. In happier circumstances, one may be inspired and transported, as in the stories of saints who were helped by giants to build a church in a single night. This would be the positive harnessing of such untamed, half-conscious emotions; then, in a white heat, man can accomplish a great task.

On the island lives a married giant couple. At the beginning of the tale, the prince's parents were not mentioned; that is, the image of the parents was missing—an unusual lacuna in a fairy tale—and therefore the giants are probably the energic equivalent, an archaic form of the parents. Since the king and queen are not present and the giants take over their role, there is no longer a ruling principle in consciousness, and it has therefore regressed into its archaic form. There is always a dominating force of some sort, and if the ruling and guiding principle wavers, then there is a throwback to earlier ways. For instance, in Switzerland the ideal of freedom was revered as a mystical bride—the ideal of social coherence without constraint—and whenever there is a threat from without, this ideal is quickened again. But in peaceful times it slips from people's grasp and they revive instead the idea of political associations. A similar state of affairs prevails now in the world at large, where giants—uncontrolled collective, emotional forces—lord it over the earth. Society is unconsciously led by primitive and archaic principles.

In the kitchen of the giant couple, Ring finds the dog called Snati-Snati, who is the complementary other side of the hero. Historically, the kitchen was the center of the house and was therefore the place of the house cults. The house gods were placed on the kitchen stove and in prehistoric times the dead were buried under the hearth. As the place where food is chemically transformed, the kitchen is analogous to the stomach. It is the center of emotion in its searing and consuming aspect and in its illuminating and warming function, both of which show that the light of wisdom only comes out of the fire of passion. When the dog is in the kitchen, this means that he represents a complex whose activity reveals itself especially in the emotional sphere.

Snati-Snati is guarded by the giants both as a sort of secret and as a sort of son. The forbidden room with its frightful secret is a widespread motif. In such a room something uncanny and formidable is usually kept, and this again represents a complex which is completely repressed and closed off—something incompatible with the attitude of consciousness. Because of this one is reluctant to approach the forbidden room, but at the same time one is fascinated and wants to enter it.

Often the figure in the forbidden room gets into a rage when someone enters; that is, the complex also opposes the opening of the door. The incompatibility sets up a resistance on both sides against being made conscious, with the result that they repel each other like two particles of the same electricity. It can therefore be said that the repression is an energic process supported from both sides. (Many psychological phenomena are best explained by assuming that psychical life has characteristics analogous to events in physics. Jung examines this analogy in detail in his essays "On the Nature of Dreams" and "On Psychic Energy."[31]

In our tale the dog responds at once to Ring's approach. He is neither a monster nor a god but stands in a good relation to man except for the fact that he is unnaturally far away from the hero. That the giants do not object to Ring's taking away the dog—that is, his easy assimilation of the contents represented by the dog—shows that there is no resistance on the part of the unconscious, and this—the fact that there is no great tension between human consciousness and the world of the instincts—gives a rough idea of the date of this tale; namely, soon after the conversion of Scandinavia to Christianity, between the eleventh and fourteenth centuries.

The hero and the dog travel to the mainland to the palace of a king, and Snati-Snati tells the prince to ask for a room in the palace for the winter. Here the king, his daughter, and the perfidious Rauder (or Raut) dwell. It should be noted that this king, not the real father of Ring, is the father of the anima and that the mother is missing—a lack that connects with the fact that both Ring and the dog are under the influence of a negative mother-image. Moreover, the precious treasures that belong to this king are no longer with him but are hoarded by a baneful giant-mother who lives with her family on a mountain.

The minister Rauder (often called Rot or Rothut—Red or Red Hat—names that hint at the violence of his emotions) is a figure frequently found in northern fairy tales. (Cf. Grimm's "Ferdinand the Faithful and Ferdinand the Unfaithful," wherein the shadow figure advises the king what the hero, his double should do.) This slanderer at the king's court is a destructive aspect of the hero's shadow—a disturbing function that sows enmity and discord. Because Prince Ring is too passive and too good, Rauder represents his as yet unassimilated dark emotions and impulses—jealousy, hatred, and murderous passion. But this evil minister has an essential function, for he creates the tasks whereby Ring is able to distinguish himself; he incites the prince to heroic action, and in this way the evil shadow has a positive value and a luciferian light-bringing quality. He is a driving force in the unconscious, which is evil only insofar as its function is not understood and which is effaced as soon as the hero wins the daughter and the kingdom. For the dark shadow to lose its power as soon as the hero triumphs is a typical *dénouement*. He would be superfluous if the hero were energetic and equal to performing his tasks. Like Mephisto for Faust, Rauder is unwittingly an instrument of growth for Ring.

This touches upon the problem of evil as seen from the standpoint of nature. As this fairy tale and others indicate, evil incitements provide us with the opportunities to increase consciousness. It seems that nature takes this view and represents it in this way. When we are able to see our own greed, jealousy, spite, hatred, and so on, then these can be turned to positive account because in such destructive emotions is stored much life, and when we have this energy at our disposal, it can be turned to positive ends.

The dominant characteristic of this false and crafty steward is envy, and envy is a misunderstood compulsion to achieve something within oneself that one has neglected. It springs from a vague awareness of a deficiency in one's character, a deficiency that needs to be realized; it points to a lack which can be filled. The object of envy embodies what one might oneself have created or achieved, and therefore it is a fault that can be remedied.

The figure of Rauder shows little that is animal-like or instinctive but rather that which is sinister and shrewd—shadow qualities of which the hero could and should be conscious, contents that should fuse with and be contained in the archetype of the hero. This brings up the following question: to what extent do such negative factors support the king's position? Sometimes they are embodied in the king, in which case he himself imposes the impossible tasks on the hero because the new system (personified by the hero) must demonstrate that it is stronger and better than the old one; in other words, that it will create a better state of collective psychic health and give a more abundant cultural life. This is the old king's secret justification for imposing formidable tasks on the one who aspires to inherit the kingdom. One can see this in the struggle between early Christianity and the old pagan gods. The early Christians felt more alive, they had greater vitality, new enthusiasm, and a hopeful attitude, and they were active socially, whereas the heathen were disillusioned and their esprit was worn out. Because of these things the issue was decided. People watch for signs of vitality and join the movement that looks as if it will make them feel better and be better. That is how a new system demonstrates its superiority and wins the anima (the king's daughter)—in other words, the souls of men.

Service at the court of a foreign king is a recurring image, and the hero who undertakes this is almost always the heir to the throne. This motif arises when the ruling principle of collective consciousness becomes oppressive and the time has come when it should abdicate.

Turning to the tasks of the hero, one finds that they are generally the work of civilizing: the taming or slaying of wild animals, agricultural labor, the building of a church in a single night, and so on. One of the tasks in the present story is the felling of trees; that is, the clearing of a place where the light of consciousness can fall into the realm of the unconscious and subdue a part of it. A wood is a region where visibility is limited, where one loses one's way, where wild animals and unexpected dangers may be present, and therefore, like the sea, it is a symbol of the unconscious. Early man lived in jungles and forests, and the making of a clearing was a cultural step. The unconscious is wild nature, which swallows up every human attempt, like the forest against which primitive man must keep eternally vigilant.

Aside from this, wood is vegetable life, an organic form that draws life directly from the earth and transforms the soil. Through plants, inorganic matter becomes living. Since plants take their nourishment in part from the mineral contents of the earth, they signify that form of life which is closely connected with inorganic matter, and this can be said to parallel the life of the body in its intimate connection with the unconscious.

In order to accomplish the difficult tasks, Prince Ring has to have the help of his other shadow side, the dog, which increasingly takes the initiative. The two become strongly allied, and the hero acquires the help of the instincts in the form of the positive shadow. On the other hand, the helpful instinct provides the hero with the sense of reality that he needs and gives him roots in this world.

Ring's second assignment is to vanquish wild bulls. The slaying of the bull was of primary importance in the Mithraic mystery rites, vestiges of which still exist in Spain and Mexico. The killing of the bull is an assertion and demonstration of the ascendancy of human consciousness over the wild, emotional animal forces. Nowadays the bull is not dominant in the unconscious psyche; on the contrary, our difficulty is to find the way back to our instinctive animal life, and in this story the hero must assert his self-control and his masculine qualities before the dog can be redeemed.

The next section of the tale has to do with the giants from whom the hero must recover the stolen treasures, and it is important that the action takes place on a mountain. In Hinduism the mountain is connected with the Mother Goddess. Being close to the heavens, it is often the place of revelation, as in the transfiguration of Christ. In many creation myths it signifies a place of orientation, for example, the initial appearance of four mountains at the cardinal points. The apostles and spiritual leaders of the church were identified with mountains by certain Fathers of the Church. The medieval author Richard de Saint Victor interprets the mountain on which Christ stands as a symbol of self-knowledge that leads to the inspired wisdom of the prophets. Often the mountain is the goal of a long quest or the site of the transition into eternity. The mountain motif also denotes the Self.

Summing up the aspects of the mountain symbolism that connect with our tale, we note that the mountain in the story has to do with the moon goddess in the person of the giant-mother. The mountain also marks the place—the point in life—where the hero, after arduous effort (climbing), becomes oriented and gains steadfastness and self-knowledge, values that develop through the effort to become conscious in the process of individuation. Actually, the mother aspect is paramount, and in relation to the problem presented by the mother, the hero must make a tremendous effort and must be able to rely on his instinct. For this reason Ring lets his dog lead him.

Self-knowledge is symbolized by the precious golden objects that the prince finds on the mountain, and this knowledge is also symbolized by the salt, which Ring tosses into the groats, inducing an agonizing thirst in the giants, so that they emerge from the cave and run to the sea one by one and are all drowned.

Salt is a part of the sea and has the inherent bitterness of the sea. The idea of bitterness is also associated with tears and with sadness, disappointment, and loss. In Latin, *sal* also means "wit" or "joke." Salt in alchemy is called "the salt of wisdom" because it endows one with a penetrating spiritual power and is a mystical world principle like sulfur and quicksilver. Thus wisdom, a skeptical turn of mind, pungent sorrow, and irony may according to Jung all be symbolized by salt. Some alchemists prescribe salt as being the only means of overcoming the devil. On the other hand, in alchemy, salt is praised as the Eros principle, and it is called "an opener and a uniter." From this we may conclude that salt symbolizes the wisdom of Eros, its bitterness together with its life-giving power—the wisdom acquired by feeling-experiences.

In the present tale, the Eros principle leads the hero on his quest, and the salt works to isolate the giants and make them beatable. The hero has a sort of spiritual attitude which is more resourceful than the slow wits of the giants.

If we sum up the aspects of the shadow in this story, we see that there are two shadow figures: the dog and Rauder—an animal double and a malicious human double, two forms of the shadow, one positive and the other negative. The dog is intimately bound up with the hero, whereas Rauder is separable and transient. The two have played out their respective roles only when the hero is joined with his anima.

Although we cannot get past the fact that the dog is an unknown part of man's psyche, a part best expressed by the image of a dog (like all symbols it is its own best expression), if we wish to circumscribe its meaning, we recall that in antiquity the dog was regarded as a guarantor of eternal life (for example, Cerberus of Hades and the images of dogs on antique Roman graves). In Egyptian mythology, the jackal-headed god Anubis is a guide into the underworld and is said to have gathered together the dismembered body of Osiris. The priest who performed the rites of mummification was costumed as an Anubis figure. In Greece, the dog belongs to the god of healing, Asklepios, because he knows how to cure himself by eating grass. The dog is usually very positive in his relation to man; he is a friend, a guardian, and a guide. But as the carrier of frenzy or madness (hydrophobia) he was also much dreaded in earlier times and was thought to bring disease and pestilence. Of all animals the dog is the most completely adapted to people, is most responsive to their moods, copies them, and understands what is expected of him. He is the essence of relationship.

Snati-Snati, however, is not really a dog, and in the end we learn that he is a prince, also called Ring and also under the spell of the giant-woman, whom they finally overcome. He could not be released until he had slept on the wedding night at the foot of the bed of a prince who bore his name, and so one can say that this dog represents an instinctive urge which later turns into a human quality. One can also say that this animal drive which needs and wants to be integrated contains a hidden strain of the hero. The dog is the hero's complementary instinctive side, whose assimilation brings the hero's realization of himself into three-dimensional life.

The shadow depicted in Rauder is sometimes replaced in other tales by two backbiting brothers of the hero, and these brothers represent tendencies toward a one-sided development which is either too "spiritual" or too instinctive. Rauder has a jealous nature, with the consequent dangerous tendency to narrow one-sidedness. He symbolizes passionate possessiveness, but he performs a positive function by imposing the impossible tasks on the hero. When the anima comes, however, he must go.

Finally he attempts to murder the hero, and then he is attacked by the dog—by an instinctive reaction that disarms him and defeats his purpose. In his attempt to murder Ring, Rauder shows his hand—and the dog bites it off. Endurance is of great importance when dealing with evil forces. The one who can hold out without losing his temper is the one who wins. There are even tales featuring a wager between the hero and the evil spirit, in which the one who is the first to let loose his emotions forfeits his life. Losing one's temper always means a lowering of consciousness, a lapse into primitive or even animal reactions.

Rauder was formidable while he pitted human shrewdness against Ring, but then his animal passion for sheer destructiveness got the better of him, and that is why he was overcome by the animal. He represents a bit of unassimilable evil in the psyche which resists sublimation and which must be thrown out. One alchemist observed that in the *prima materia* there is a certain intractable amount of *terra damnata* (accursed earth) that defies all efforts at transformation and must be rejected. Not all dark impulses lend themselves to redemption; certain ones, soaked in evil, cannot be allowed to break loose and must be severely repressed. What is against nature, against the instincts, has to be stopped by main force and eradicated. The expression "assimilation of the shadow" is meant to apply to childish, primitive, undeveloped sides of one's nature, depicted in the image of the child or the dog or the stranger. But there are deadly germs that can destroy the human being and must be resisted, and their presence means that one must be hard from time to time and not accept everything that comes up from the unconscious.

Snati-Snati turns out to be a prince, and one wonders why he had been transformed into a dog. This has to do with the dual nature of the instinct, which is an ambiguous phenomenon. Biologists regard it as the meaningful but unreflective mode of behavior of animals, as an inborn pattern of behavior which only the higher animals are able to modify. This pattern consists of two factors: a physical activity and a picture or image of the activity, this being necessary to energize the activity. The image works as a catalyst for the physical action and also represents the meaning of the action. Normally the two factors exist and work together, but they can be separated. If another image is substituted for the original one, the instinctive behavior can attach to the new image. Woodcocks, for instance, which were hatched out in a stove addressed their mating play to the wooden clogs of the human attendants, the clogs for them being "imprinted" with the mother-image. These images or pictures are what we call archetypal images.

Snati-Snati, therefore, is the psychic pattern or image in which the course of self-realization appears first as an instinct, but within which lies a human complementary side. The dog form of this drive derives from a false conception of individuation, a collective misconception entertained by consciousness: hence the curse of the stepmother.

In every age there are widespread collective convictions about what constitutes the path of individuation. For example, in the Middle Ages the idea that people should model their entire lives and their inner conduct on the life of Christ is what we would call individuation. Today there is a current notion that we are healed, fulfilled, and made complete when our physical instincts are normal, especially the sexual instinct. According to the Freudians, the root of all evil is sexual repression; if the amatory functions take their natural course, then everything is resolved and in order. Devotees of this belief bend their energy to this purpose but often find that they cannot get rid of their inhibitions in this way. Exactly because it is overvalued, the spontaneous thing cannot happen naturally. People saddle the instinct with psychological expectations and put a mystical idea of redemption into a biological fact. Thus something which does not belong to the animal sphere has been projected into it. Other examples of this sort of mixing can be found in the idea that the full meaning of life is celebrated when a communist or other social order enters one's country and that one's highest ideals are then fulfilled (or the warrior ideal of some cultures, as revived by the Nazis). The Nazis put the ideal of individuation into their program, but that ideal was spoiled and made soulless by false collective interpretations. The youth of the country gave to it devotion, intensity, and the willingness to sacrifice because they identified it with what we call individuation. Idealism and willingness to sacrifice are admirable in themselves, but they were given a false direction. Because the millennium is originally a symbol of the Self, it caught their imagination. Or take the fantastic idea of women having children for the Führer. The underlying idea is that feminine productivity should be under a spiritual guiding principle, that women should not produce children like animals but under the aegis of a guiding life principle. But this was falsified by projection and the wrong conception of spiritual development put too much weight on materialism, and thereby the women degraded themselves.

When symbolic factors are repressed, they glut the instincts, and therefore they must be separated out so that the genuine instincts can function without being overloaded. As I have said, when people overemphasize sexuality, they put something in the animal sphere which does not belong there, and a real effort must be made to integrate the shadow in order to allow the instincts to function in some sort of harmony.

If we depict the journey of the prince in a maplike fashion, his route turns out to be circular—like a ring—because the fourth station is secretly identical with the first, for both are ruled by the stepmother. (See diagram.)

The hero ultimately winds up at the place from which he started, but his circuit has netted him the dog (Ring 2nd), the princess, and the kingdom. The whole process is a continuous adding on, a process of increasing completion, which is ordered like a mandala. This is a typical pattern in fairy tales.

The course of these four stations leads deeper and deeper into the unconscious. Between stages II and III the hero leads the way, but between III and IV the dog guides the hero. At the fourth station, all evil elements disappear: the giant-couple on the island die of old age, the other giants, including the witch-giantess, are killed, and Rauder is hanged. Stages I and IV have a secret identity

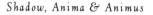

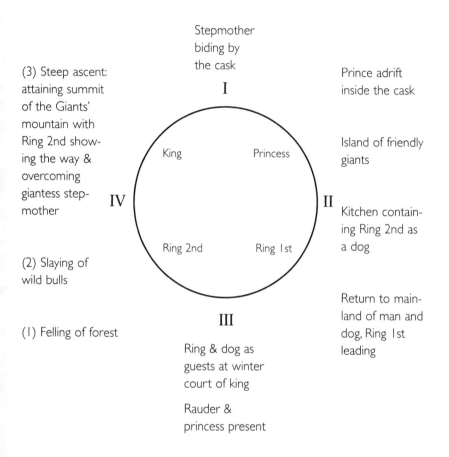

Stepmother
biding by
the cask

I

Prince adrift
inside the cask

(3) Steep ascent:
attaining summit
of the Giants'
mountain with
Ring 2nd show-
ing the way &
overcoming
giantess step-
mother

Island of friendly
giants

King   Princess

IV   II

Ring 2nd   Ring 1st

Kitchen contain-
ing Ring 2nd as
a dog

(2) Slaying of
wild bulls

III

Return to main-
land of man and
dog, Ring 1st
leading

(1) Felling of forest

Ring & dog as
guests at winter
court of king

Rauder &
princess present

because they have to do with the same psychic complex realized on
different levels. The hind, the seaside witch, and the giantess are
secretly one and the same figure—the one who persecutes the two
Rings.

The fourth stage also fulfills what was latent: marriage with the
anima and the emancipation of the second prince from bondage to
his dog form (after having been freed earlier from bondage to the
forbidden kitchen). Only with the attainment of the Self are the
shadow and the anima really won because only then does the situa-

tion become stabilized. The fourth-station structure occurs frequently in fairy tales that feature royal personages, and these tales generally conclude with a group formed by four persons.

This fairy tale in its entirety represents an *energic process of transformation* within the Self, and one may compare this to the transformations that take place within an atom or its nucleus.

To sum up what we discussed, the fairy tale does not represent a personal shadow figure, but the collective shadow of the collective hero figure. It consists of an animal double which is positive, and an evildoer who is destructive. Actually, the animal double is more an undeveloped aspect of the Self.

The Challenge of the Anima

The Bewitched Princess

A man had a son called Peter who wished to remain at home no longer, so he asked for his inheritance of twenty shillings and departed. On his way he came upon a dead man lying in the fields who had been left unburied because he was poor, and Peter, having a good heart, gave his twenty shillings to provide the man with a decent burial.

Continuing on his way, Peter was joined by a stranger, and they decided to travel together. They came to a town where everything was veiled in black as a sign of mourning for the princess, who was bewitched by an evil mountain spirit. She put three riddles to each one of her suitors, and if he failed to guess every one, she killed him. Although none had been able to redeem her by guessing the riddles and many had lost their lives, Peter decided to try. His companion, who was really the ghost of the buried man, offered to help him. He strapped great wings on Peter's back, gave him an iron rod, and told him to fly behind the princess that night wherever she might go and to beat her with the rod. Above all, Peter was to take in whatever she said to the mountain spirit whose captive she was.

After nightfall Peter flew to the windowsill of the princess's room, and when she threw open the window and flew away he followed, pummeling her with his rod. They came to a high mountain, which opened, and both entered a large hall where Peter saw a few scattered stars in the darkness overhead and an altar near the entrance. Then the princess ran to the arms of the mountain spirit, who had a snow-white beard and eyes like burning coals. She reported that another suitor would arrive the following day and wanted to know what riddle to confound him with. The mountain spirit swore that she must kill this man. "The more human blood you drink, the more you are really mine," he said, "and the purer in my eyes you become. Think of your father's white horse and charge the suitor to tell you what you are thinking of." After this she flew back and went to bed.

The next morning Peter presented himself and found her sitting on her sofa, quite melancholy but looking mild and fair. You would scarcely have guessed that she had already sent nine men to their death. She asked, "What am I thinking of?" Without hesitation Peter responded, "Of your father's white horse." She turned pale and bade him return the following day for the next riddle.

That night Peter again found the princess, but when he entered the mountain hall, he saw on the altar a prickly fish and the moon shining above it. This time the princess was thinking of her father's sword, and Peter again divined the answer at once.

On the third night the spirit-companion equipped Peter with a sword and two iron rods. This time he found that there was a fiery wheel on the altar beside the prickly fish and overhead a sun so bright that he had to hide behind the altar to avoid being seen. He heard the mountain spirit decide that the riddle should concern the mountain spirit's head. "Because no mortal can think of it," he assured the princess. So when she left, Peter resolutely lopped off the head of the mountain spirit, took it with him, and pursued the princess, striking her with both iron rods.

The next morning when she asked him to guess the riddle, Peter threw the head of the mountain spirit at her feet, saying, "That is what you are thinking of." The princess, torn between terror and joy, fainted, and when she recovered, she consented to marry her suitor.

On the wedding day, Peter's companion cautioned him to have a large vessel full of water ready when he went to bed that night. "And when the bride gets up, toss her into it," the companion said. "Then she will turn into a raven. Put this raven back in the water, and she will become a dove. Plunge the dove under water, and she will come out in her true form, as gentle as an angel." The companion then disappeared.

Peter acted on this advice, redeemed the princess, and later became king.[32]

In a parallel Norwegian tale, the following substitutions and variations occur: The man whose burial the hero pays for is a wine merchant who was wont to dilute his wine with water. The mountain spirit is a troll to whom the princess rides every night on a male goat. Instead of guessing, the hero must produce the objects she is thinking of, which are a pair of scissors, a golden spool, and the troll's head. Before they reach the domain of the princess, the hero and his companion have to overcome three witches, and then they have a river to cross. The ghost companion makes the crossing possible by throwing the golden spool to the opposite side of the river, and the spool then returns by itself. In this way golden threads unwind back and forth until a bridge is spun, sturdy enough to walk across. Finally, after winning the princess, the hero must bathe her in milk and beat her until she loses her troll skin; otherwise, she would have slain him. In return for his companion's help, the hero had agreed to surrender one half of all that he gained, so after five years the companion turns up to exact payment, and he asks the hero to divide his child in two. But when the companion sees that the hero is willing to perform the sacrifice, he releases him from his obligation and confides that he himself may now return to heaven, having cleared his own debt to the hero.

The corpse that the hero finds is usually that of some poor wretch who died in debt or the corpse of a criminal or a suicide. In the parallel tale, the shadow is either human or spiritual and does not appear in animal form as in the story of Prince Ring. Instead, he is a morally inferior person, a cheat who has diluted the wine.

In the main version, the shadow lacked life energy—money is energy—and is therefore impoverished and must come into his own again. He represents an unlived part of the life within the hero, potential qualities that have not yet entered his character and his actions. Autonomous complexes often thrive without the ego suspecting that they exist, and sooner or later they will be constellated and will appear, usually in an unpleasant form at first.

If one were Peter in the story, one might easily assume that one was not responsible for the corpse, but when it is one's own shadow, one is responsible. Only a conscious and responsible attitude transforms the shadow into a friend. Giving one's money for the burial of the corpse means that one has concern for the shadow and devotes energy to it. To those who refuse to do this, the shadow is deceptive and lives by cheating—by mixing water with the wine. The nature of this shadow is dishonest: by substituting ordinary water for the more valuable, effort-costing wine, he seeks to get more for less. His crime lies in shirking work.

In antiquity it was considered an act of hubris to drink pure wine without diluting it with water, except in the Dionysian mysteries, where it meant spiritual exaltation. But this practice was ceremonial and exceptional and did not apply to everyday consumption. In the Christian symbolism of the Mass, wine represents Christ's blood, or more exactly, Christ's divine nature, and the water his common human nature (and the bread his body). I cite this only to point out that historically, wine was regarded as being spiritual and water as being common.

The guilt of the dead man was that in everyday life he blurred the divine and the human by mixing what should be discriminated. The act of mixing can be forgiven, but the dishonesty lies in his palming it off as genuine and unadulterated. People who are led by the shadow cheat themselves by thinking their motives are highly moral, while in fact they are crude drives for power. The shadow mixes things in an unclean way, mixes up facts and opinions, for instance. People fool themselves that sexual fantasies are mystical experiences. One should call a thing what it is and not pretend a physical thing is spiritual. If one unites wine and water, it should be done consciously and not in an underhanded way. The shadow gets hold of a good idea and carries it out on the wrong level, on an archaic level. When one is unaware of the shadow, it falsifies the personality.

Getting more for less has also its psychological implications. People avoid the difficult individual way. Men frequently have a shady corner in which to arrange a deal the easy way, and women who are in love or are jealous know how to make scenes in order to get their own way. Such behavior is a common human failing because the shadow is a low fellow and acts in this fashion. If he can get returns without hard work, he cannot help not working. To be able not to go the easy way is a sign of great self-discipline and culture.

In the initial situation in our tale there is also a lack of psychic energy, and this creates a sort of greed and causes men to cheat.

One who is really fascinated by the inner life has no energy or time for deliberate conniving or fraudulent maneuvers. But as long as the anima is unredeemed, life does not flow, and this locks up energy in evil and greedy tendencies.

Because the shadow is a part of the psyche which is not understood and because it has been spurned, it kills itself. If one goes too far in repressing the shadow, if one is too hard and too severe over too long a time, an unlived complex will die. This is the aim of the ascetic. When the hero drops the corpse onto the floor— that is, into reality—the shadow vanishes as a corpse and reappears as a ghost. It returns in the aspect of a spirit, so there is still a shadow problem but on a better level.

The nature of the hero also reveals the nature of the shadow. Peter is not a king's son but an ordinary lad, the anonymous common man. (Often this kind of hero does not even have a name.) He represents the average man who is also an aspect of the Self—the Anthropos—the eternal human being in common yet eternal form. (Compare Christ, who is often called *Knecht* in German, which means servant.) The shadow figure has a compensatory function and is the completion of the hero. The path of this Everyman, Peter, leads from the common form to the special royal form, whose meaning was discussed above.

The realization of the Self can be experienced through such widely different classes of heroes as prince or common stable boy. We see, for instance, that young people often identify themselves with an "inner prince" or a supernatural creature. Many others want above all to be ordinary and like everyone else. Each level yearns secretly for the other, and both types are really two sides of the Anthropos, the cosmic Man. The unconscious insists on both sides because, paradoxically, individuation means to become more individual and at the same time more generally human.

The hero often appears in the role of a deserter. He has left the collective order and is thrown into a special destiny. In our tale the shadow is transformed into an otherworldly spirit. He becomes the servant-companion of the hero, and he rounds out the boyish naiveté of the hero by his skill and knowledge. Because the hero is too low, the shadow is spiritual; Ring, being a prince, was high up, so his shadow was an animal.

The hero gives his whole heritage for the burial. This is far beyond what is customary and even beyond the means of the hero himself—a typical heroic attitude. The shadow is disposed of by burial so that it ceases to make any further claims upon human life. After this, it does not come back into life but is transformed into a spirit in the realm where it is at rest.

Providing for the burial of the shadow has a double aspect: the hero gives money (i.e., energy) and he frees himself of the shadow disturbance. To recognize the shadow is to be prepared to keep it in its place. In this tale the shadow is allowed to carry out its own purposes, and from this comes its spiritualization. When the shadow is only half-conscious it is most disturbing and indeterminate—neither fish nor fowl. The spiritualization occurs because the newly acquired shadow-companion is instrumental in accomplishing the tasks and becomes an arranger of fate. He becomes a figure more like Mephistopheles in Faust, a nature spirit or symbol of the dark side of the Self. Only if one throws a shadow is one real. The shadow plunges man into the immediacy of situations here and now and thus creates the real biography of the human being, who is always inclined to assume that he is only what he thinks he is. It is the biography created by the shadow that counts.

Only later, when the shadow has been somewhat assimilated, can the ego partially rule its own fate. Then, however, another content of the unconscious, the Self, takes over most of this fate-arranging function, and that is why the shadow-companion in our story disappears later.

In our tale the hero is completely goalless. He has no commitments at home, no specific destination abroad. This is a good precondition for the heroic action—a point that is frequently stressed. He gets bored at home, takes his heritage and sallies forth, all of which indicates that energy has already left consciousness and has reinforced the unconscious. One can only discover the mystery of the unconscious as a reality when one is naively curious, not when one wants to harness its power for the furtherance of some conscious design.

As soon as the first step is taken in relation to the shadow problem, the anima is activated. In the Norwegian parallel she has a troll skin; that is, she belongs to an older, more primitive order of life and has a heathen character. The anima often appears uncanny and troll-like in Nordic myth, and then she represents a challenge to the traditional Christian life. In order to amplify this pagan aspect of the anima, let us digress from our story and consider a couple of Scandinavian tales. The following is the story of a man crippling himself by refusing to have anything to do with his pagan anima.

The Secret Church

The schoolmaster of Etnedal loved to spend his holidays by himself in a hut in the mountains. Once he heard the church bells, and since there was no church nearby, he looked about him, astonished, and saw a group of people in Sunday clothes trooping along in front of his hut on a path which had not been there before. He followed them and came to a little wooden church which was also new to him. He was very impressed by the old pastor's sermon, but he noticed that the name of Jesus Christ was never mentioned and there was no blessing at the end.

After the service, the schoolmaster was invited to the pastor's house, and over a cup of tea the daughter told him that her father was quite old and asked if the schoolmaster would be willing to be his successor when he died. The schoolmaster begged to be allowed to think the matter over for a time. The daughter said that she would give him a whole year. As soon as she said this, he found himself back in the woods among familiar surroundings. He felt puzzled for a few days and then the matter slipped his mind.

The following year he was again in his mountain hut and, noticing that the roof was weathering away, he climbed up with his ax to do some repair work. Suddenly he became aware of someone coming down the path in front of the hut. It was the pastor's daughter. Seeing him, she asked if he was willing to accept the pastorship. He replied, "I cannot answer for it to God and my conscience, so I must refuse." At that moment the girl disappeared and he inadvertantly brought the ax down upon his own knee, with the result that he was a cripple for the rest of his days.[33]

This tale shows that repressing the anima for conventional reasons results in actual psychic self-mutilation. If one gets too high up (up on the roof), one loses one's natural contact with the earth (the leg). This anima figure is a heathen demon.

Here is another example which illustrates the unfortunate consequences resulting from an inappropriate way of coping with the problem of the heathen anima.

The Wood Woman

A woodcutter once saw a beautiful woman sewing in the woods, and her spool of thread rolled to his feet. She bade him return it to her and he did, although he knew that this meant he was submitting to her charm. On the following night, though he was careful to sleep in the midst of his comrades, she came and fetched him. They went into the mountains where everything was quiet and beautiful.

There he became infected with madness. One day when the troll-woman brought him something to eat, he saw that she had a cow's tail, and he made it fast in a split tree trunk; then he wrote the name of Christ on it. She fled and her tail was left in the trunk, and he saw that his meal was only cow dung.

Later he came to a hut in the woods and saw a woman and child, both with a cow's tail. The woman said to the child, "Go bring your father a drink of beer." The man fled in horror. Later he returned safely to his village, but he remained a bit queer for the rest of his days.[34]

This tale shows the dangerous spell that the anima casts on a man whose ego and willpower are frail. To yield to her means losing human contact and going completely wild, while to repress her means a loss of spirit and of energy.

The same type of dangerous anima figure appears in a story of the South American Cherente Indians:

The Star

A young man who was living in the bachelors' hut looked with longing each night at a brilliant star in the heavens and thought, "What a pity I cannot carry you about in my bottle all day and admire you." One night when he awoke from a deep dream about the star, he saw a girl by his bed with beautiful, deeply shining eyes. She told him that she was the very star that attracted him and that she had the ability to make herself small enough to dwell in the bottle and thus they might be together.

They lived together by night, but during the day, while he pocketed her in his bottle, her eyes blazed like a wildcat's. The young man soon became very unhappy, and his fears were realized one day when she told him that she was leaving. She touched a tree with a magic rod so that it towered up into the skies and she ascended to heaven. Against his will the young man followed her, although she begged him not to, and high up in the tree he discovered a festival in full swing. He was alarmed to observe skeletons dancing in a circle, and he fled in terror. The girl appeared again and told him to take a bath of purification, but it was of no avail. When he touched earth again, he had a splitting headache and soon died.[35]

The Indians seem aware of the alluring danger of the archetypal images of the collective unconscious and their power to take one away from reality. They discovered that although the stars seem to promise happiness, there is no bliss in heaven.

The anima is portrayed as a miraculous spirit and at the same time as a ferocious animal. She often appears as deathly and dreadful, and when this is the case it is important to keep consciousness away from the unconscious. That is why, as a warning, the unconscious is depicted as a mortal danger. This motif is common in primitive tales. Then the hero must guard himself against exposure to the poisonous contents and not give himself up to anything that has a strange fascination over him, neither to fantasies from within nor to any dangerous and fascinating pursuits from without. So the anima has to be corked up sometimes, her powers reduced and confined, especially in an age of early culture. This is the intentional devaluation of a complex, and therefore the anima appears as a malicious, blazing-eyed animal. Her reaction is evoked by the hero's conscious attitude, but at night she resumes her divine form.

The Christian religion also uses a "bottle" for imprisoning the anima in order to limit and hold back explosive forces, namely, the cult of the Virgin, which serves as a vessel for the mother- and anima-images of man. While this conscious restraint is often necessary, there is danger in prolonging it beyond its season. It is a matter of feeling and of timing in order to desist before the unconscious gets too much cut off and dams up too much explosive power.

In "The Bewitched Princess" the hero must surmount certain trials before he reaches the anima, while in the alternative version the hero and his companion are pursued by three witches. Frequently witches are initial anima manifestations and often resemble the mother-image, like the stepmother in "Prince Ring."

Peter's companion hurls a spool of golden thread across the river to form a bridge. After the two have run across, they dismantle it in time to forestall the witches' crossing behind them, and so the witches go down to a watery death. This golden thread is a secret link with the meaningfulness of the unconscious. It is the invisible tie that threads things together, the thread of destiny which is woven by our unconscious projections.

In this story the companion is a suprapersonal guide to destiny, and it is he who has the thread and who throws it. The spool, bouncing back and forth like the shuttle of a loom, balances at a perilous stage between the uncertain present and the immediate future until the bridge to what is to come is sturdy enough. In this way one may throw projections which make it possible for him to cross over to a new inner realm. Often there is an oscillation between the opposites until a stability is achieved whereby one can cross over; that is, one can change the inner attitude.

The hero arrives at the city, which is in mourning for the bewitched captive princess, and learns that several princes have perished trying to save her. The anima is under a spell and is trapped because a process in the unconscious is not understood: hence her riddles, which must first be answered. The riddles of the anima mean that she does not understand herself and is not yet in her right place within the total psychic system. Moreover, she cannot solve this problem by herself but needs the help of consciousness. On the other hand, the hero is in the same fix because he too has not yet found his place and he too does not know himself. Thus the riddle is something between both of them, something they have to solve together. It is the riddle of right relationship. The riddle recalls the Sphinx, also half-animal, like the girl dressed in a troll skin in the Norwegian version. The classical question of the Sphinx in the Oedipus myth concerns the *being* of man, which is the great mystery we cannot yet understand.

When the anima problem is not understood, the anima, like the princess, who is a creature of moods, either sulks and becomes silent and sullen or becomes angry and hysterical. The anima poses a moral problem, although she herself is amoral. She can be counted on to set the most confused and intricate problems, but she is released when the hero lives up to his name, and then she guides him to higher consciousness.

The shadow companion equips the hero with wings so that now he can fly in the world of the anima. This means a new conscious attitude, a certain spiritualization, because wings belong to a fantasy being rather than an earthly being. The ability to go into the realms of fantasy is essential to the finding of the anima; one must be freed from profane reality, at least to the extent of trying to fantasize. Detachment is also needed, objective observation with open eyes, a willingness to observe without interfering and judging.

The companion also equips the hero with a rod, a means of criticism to soften the powerful effect of the anima. The rod signifies the implacability which is necessary in order to punish the anima for her murderous and demonic behavior. The hero must follow her, stay with her, and yet criticize her negative side. Though he beats her with the rod, it must not be hard enough to beat her into the earth.

The princess, like the unconscious, is a piece of nature and therefore undiscriminating. Consciousness surpasses her in the ability to adapt to a situation because consciousness is normally more cool and resourceful; it has patience and appreciates distinctions. But as a piece of nature the unconscious is unconfined, turbulent, and elementally powerful. The not-yet-human impulses of the unconscious often appear, therefore, as giants who represent the uprush of instinctive power. Despite their might, they are easily fooled, and therefore there needs to be wisdom to give direction to this energy.

The mountain that Peter and his companion fly to signifies the effort toward self-knowledge. It is here that the hero must learn the anima's secret.

The mountain spirit belongs to the archetype of the wise old man, who frequently has a daughter in thrall in a sort of incestuous relationship. That he has an altar suggests secret religious ceremonies, and he may be regarded as a kind of priest. At the same time, there is something chthonic and underworldly about this "father" of the anima. He is analogous to the dragon in the Russian parallel to the tale of the three feathers—a dark, pagan god. Often he assigns insurmountable tasks to the hero who wishes to win his "daughter," and here the anima presents riddles that he has devised. The mountain spirit behind the anima represents a secret, meaningful plan or image governing her, which means that behind the anima is the possibility of a further inner development of the hero. The anima's "father" is the greater wisdom which is in touch with the laws of the unconscious. That the mountain spirit is a superpersonal force is indicated by the altar and by the fish being worshiped in his domain. He denotes a part of the spirit of nature and a wisdom that have been neglected in civilized development. In the Norwegian version the mountain spirit is personified by a troll who is the lover of the princess, and the troll has a he-goat, often a theriomorphic form of the devil. The troll is afraid of the hero.

The idea of a spirit is originally closely allied to the thought that the soul lingers on after death. The idea of spirit moves between its subjective and objective aspects. Primitives experience spirit as a wholly other, purely objective occurrence, whereas we tend to believe that a spiritual experience is subjective. But spirit originally was—and still is to a great extent—an autonomous archetypal factor.

In fairy tales, according to Jung, the old man is usually a helpful figure who appears when the hero is in difficulty and needs counsel and guidance. He represents the concentration of mental power and purposeful reflection; even more important, he introduces genuinely objective thinking. Thus the symbol of the spirit has neutral or positive or negative aspects. If the old man in the tale is only positive or only negative, he represents but half of the nature of the archetypal old man, and in this connection one thinks of the double aspect of Merlin. In the present tale the old man is the animus of the anima, so to speak, and this means an objective spirit behind the anima.

Such figures of old men in a mountain are a folklore motif; for instance, Barbarossa,[36] or Mercurius in alchemy,[37] who is now a boy, now an old man, now destructive, now inspiring, and whose character depended upon the attitude of the alchemist. In alchemical tales the student of alchemy often seeks the truth in the bowels of the mountains, where he meets an old man, a Hermes-Mercurius figure. This spirit is the goal and at the same time the inspiration that leads to the goal. He is called "the friend of God" and has the key or the book and preserves all the secrets. At a later date the alchemists asked themselves how this Mercurius figure was related to the Christian God and found that he was a chthonic reflection of the God-image.

The temple in the middle of the mountain is also a frequently occurring motif in European fairy tales. A manmade edifice in the mountain means a structured form in the unconscious; that is, a cultural development that was suddenly uprooted or dropped without having undergone a transition into the mainstream of culture.

Such an edifice symbolizes a broken-off cultural shoot, an interruption of cultural development like the sudden cutting-off of alchemy and of the qualitative view of nature (in favor of an exclusively quantitative approach) in the seventeenth century. This leaves the former development intact but merely as a piece of tradition, while its effectiveness is sealed off.

The anima is bound to the mountain spirit because he has the secret which would make her live. Our modern consciousness has not given the soul enough room or enough life and attempts to exclude it. Therefore, the anima clings to the mountain spirit because she feels that he holds the promise of a richer life for her; this has to do with his being pagan and the fact that the pagan *Weltanschauung,* in certain respects, gave the anima in man a more abundant chance to live.

The clue to the mountain spirit's being a non-Christian figure perhaps lies in the date of the origin of the tale. Fairy tales, like archetypal dreams, correspond to a slow, deep, progressive process in the collective unconscious. Their meaning takes a long time to strike root and penetrate consciousness, so one can only date them within a margin of about three hundred years. This tale must belong to a later time than the Renaissance, a period which shows the application of Christian principles to earthly things; for instance, Johann Kepler assigned to the universe the picture of the Trinity; for him, the three dimensions of space were an image of the Trinity, the Godhead being a sphere of which the Father is the center, the Son the superficies or outer side, and the Holy Ghost the radii. According to Kepler, all creatures long to be spheres— that is, to emulate God. The whole of the Enlightenment, so called, can be described as being based on a trinitarian form of thinking, an incomplete standpoint which excluded the problem of evil and the irrational elements in nature. Opposition developed between this new style of thinking and the former way of thought. The new thinking, because of its estrangement from the irrational and from the soul, was and is quite as one-sided as the former. In order to counterbalance the new tendency, the inheritors of the traditional way asserted its tenets more loudly. The two sides set up separate camps, and neither can complement the other's distortions.

The first object of thought that the mountain spirit proposes to the princess in order to baffle the hero is her father's white horse, and here a new figure and a king, the real father of the anima, is introduced indirectly. One thinks of Sleipnir, Wotan's horse, which represents the positive energy behind the archetype of the Wotan image. As I suggested earlier, the king sometimes symbolizes a moribund system of spiritual and worldly order. Possibly the father of the anima may stand for a worn-out Christian *Weltanschauung,* in contrast to which the renegade mountain spirit plays a parallel role as a father. The latter is an exuberant upwelling of libido that stirs in the unconscious—the living archetype, which is threatening because it has been repressed. The hero must be on his guard against the opposites denoted by the two kingly figures, which like all extreme opposites are mysteriously one. The white horse is a symbol for the unconscious powers at the disposal of consciousness.[38]

The second object that the princess must think of is the sword, which stands for justice, authority, decision (consider Alexander's splitting of the Gordian knot), and discrimination, both in understanding and in willing. The motif of the sword plays a great role in alchemy.[39] The dragon, for example, is cut up by the sword, and this signifies the attempt to discriminate the instincts so that undefined unconscious contents are made more definite. One must cut the *prima materia* "with its own sword": a conscious decision is necessary in order to free the libido offered by the unconscious. In other words, the decision about which course to take has to be made by the conscious personality and is an essential precondition for the unconscious to go ahead. "Take the sword! Cleave the dragon!"—then something will develop. In the ceremony of the Mass the sword symbolizes the Logos, and in the Apocalypse it is the Logos functioning as God's decisive Word, judging the world. The flaming sword placed before the garden of Eden is explained in alchemy as the wrath of the Old Testament God. In the Gnostic system of Simon Magus the flaming sword was interpreted as the passion which separates the earth from Paradise. The sword has also a negative meaning; namely, to be destructive and to cut off possibilities of life. Like the horse, the sword signifies libido from the unconscious, a portion of psychic power. The horse and the sword are in this way linked, but the sword is an instrument made by man and the horse is instinctive libido.

The third object is the head of the mountain spirit, a thing of which no mortal being can conceive. The Greek alchemists declared that the great secret lies in the brain. In the *Timaeus* Plato also pointed out that the head repeats the ball-form of the universe, or of God. Similarly, it carries man's divine secrets. This is probably one of the reasons why primitives frequently have cults of the head. The Sabians, for instance, steeped a "golden-headed" (blond) man in oil, then cut off his head and used it as an oracle. The alchemists called themselves "children of the golden head," and the alchemist Zosimos taught that the Omega (Ω) is the great secret. In alchemy the head is also a symbol of the Self. With the help of the head we have the key to the solution of inner problems. The head was later interpreted as *essence* or *meaning*. About the head it was said that "no one could think of it," meaning that it is beyond human ability to fathom this concealed mystery. In our story, it is the head that propounds the riddles and is therefore at the bottom of all the riddles of the anima. Thus the hero's acquisition of the head is the solution of his problem, because possessing it, he is then able to understand his inner psychic processes.

The three objects of thought—the horse, the sword, and the head—express the fact that the old conscious system has a certain will and energy, although its dynamism and meaning have reverted to the unconscious. There is therefore the split between conscious energy and unconscious meaning, which is a primary problem of our day.

Let us now consider the symbols found in the temple of the mountain spirit. On the hero's first trip there are only stars, and the hall is dark and the altar bare. The random stars are latent, indefinitely dispersed germs of consciousness.

On the second trip the moon is shining and a prickly fish lies on the altar. The moon, a symbol of the feminine principle, signifies a feminine attitude toward the inner and the outer worlds, one of acceptance, a receptive registering of what goes on. In some Chinese poems the moon brings repose and calm after a previous struggle.

The Greek philosopher Anaximander suggested that man was descended from a prickly fish. The fish is famous as a Christian symbol; the apostles were called "fishers of men," and Christ himself (*ichthys*) is symbolized by the fish and was so celebrated in the eucharistic meal of fishes. Both Christ and the fish are symbols of the Self. Christ draws the projection of the fish symbol out of nature, unburdening nature and concentrating it upon himself. The fish also plays a prominent role in astrology since it is the zodiacal sign that governs the first two thousand years of the Christian era. But in this sign there are two fishes, one vertical, one horizontal, the one symbolizing Christ, the other anti-Christ. The prickly fish in our tale would seem to point to the anti-Christ as a central unconscious content, but devilish. It is unapproachable, a prickly, slippery content of the unconscious which is hard and dangerous to reach. In the Middle Ages the fish was thought to be a symbol of earthly pleasure "because they are so greedy"; perhaps also because

Leviathan was a fish-monster. Jewish tradition asserts that the pious will eat Leviathan as a eucharistic meal on Doomsday. Leviathan being pure food, this means immortality. So we can see a certain ambivalence concerning the meaning of the fish.

In India, too, the fish is connected with the savior symbol. The god Manu transformed himself into a fish and saved the holy books from the flood. In alchemy, a "round fish in the middle of the sea" with no bones and a wonderful fatness is frequently mentioned, and later this fish was connected with a glowing fish which causes fever. The nettle—fire in the sea—was interpreted by the alchemists as a symbol of divine love or hellish fire. These disparate aspects are generally combined in alchemistic symbolism. While Christianity does not permit any marriage of heaven and hell, alchemy is given to paradoxical thought.

Psychologically the fish is a distant, inaccessible content of the unconscious, a sum of potential energy loaded with possibilities but with a lack of clarity. It is a libido symbol for a relatively uncharacterized and unspecified amount of psychic energy, the direction and development of which are not yet outlined. The ambivalence regarding the fish derives from its being a content below the threshold of consciousness.

On the hero's third trip the hall is brilliantly lit by the rays of a sun. (The change of objects seen by the hero suggests a gradual lightening of the unconscious until clear discernment is attained.) A midnight sun inside the mountain recalls the midnight sun shining from below that Apuleius saw in the kingdom of the dead.[40] Not only does the ego carry light but the unconscious itself has a "latent consciousness." This midnight sun is probably the original form of consciousness—a collective consciousness, not an ego consciousness. Primitives and children experience this—a knowledge of *what is known,* not a matter of "what I know." The light in the unconscious is first an uncentered, diffused haze. Our creation myth divides the creation of light into two stages: first the birth of light in general, then the birth of the sun. In Genesis, God creates light on the first day, but not until the fourth day does he create the sun and moon.

On the altar lies a fiery wheel. In India the wheel is a symbol of power and victory, a guide to power and the Way.[41] It is the wheel of redemption, moving the right way along the right line, and symbolizing the gradual intensifying of religious consciousness. In later times the wheel assumes a more sinister aspect as the wheel of rebirth, the senseless circular repetition of life processes from which one should try to escape. In either case the wheel symbolizes the self-moving power of the unconscious; that is, the Self. To move in rhythm with the movement of the psyche, the wheel, is the goal of the Indian. His aim is to keep in touch with the "course" given by the Self. But the Self may become a negative, torturing factor if its intentions are misunderstood; then the riddles go unanswered. In Babylonian times, the horoscope or astrological wheel of birth marked the appearance of the fatal wheel whereby man is caught in the wheel of his own destiny. Homage was paid to Christ as the only one who could destroy the wheel of birth by giving spiritual rebirth to the faithful. Again, in the Middle Ages Fortuna had a wheel, a kind of roulette wheel, which expressed the reckless working of blind fate upon men who are simply caught in their own unconsciousness. The alchemists often saw their work as a circular process of continual purification. The circular movement of the alchemical wheel creates a unification of the opposites: heaven becomes earthly and earth becomes heavenly. For the alchemists this was a positive symbol. Even God has been symbolized by the wheel. Niklaus von der Flüe, the Swiss mystic and saint, saw a terrifying vision of God which he portrayed as covered by a wheel. In this way he sought to soften the terrible God he had experienced and make him more acceptable and understandable.

In a Caucasian tale in which God kills a berserk hero by sending a fiery wheel against him which smashes and burns him, the wheel expresses the avenging, ominous side of the Divinity. At midsummer festivals throughout the entire Germanic agricultural region, people roll fiery wheels down the mountains. While this can be explained as a relic of a ritual attempt to support and strengthen the sun, it may also be connected with the sun as the symbol of the source of consciousness in the unconscious. A popular belief in Germanic folklore speaks of unreleased souls spinning about like fiery wheels.

The wheel of fire refers to the spontaneous movement of the psyche which manifests itself as passion or as an emotional impulse—a spontaneous uprush from the unconscious that sets one on fire. When this happens, one may say, "That idea kept on turning in my head like a wheel." Similarly, the revolving wheel illustrates the senseless circular motion of a neurotic consciousness. This happens when one has lost his connection with the inner life and is cut off from the individual meaning of his life.

In our tale the wheel in its roundness is analogous to the mountain spirit's head—a symbol of the Self but in its dark aspect. A South American Indian tale illustrates the idea that the head may have a thoroughly destructive aspect: a skull begins to roll in an uncanny way, acquires wings and claws and becomes a demonic, murderous thing, preying on men and devouring everything. This has to do with the separation of head from body and the autonomy of the head. The violent wrenching of head from body is psychologically fatal.

Like vampires, the anima and the mountain spirit love the blood of their victims. The vampire motif is worldwide. Vampires are the spirits of the dead in Hades to whom Odysseus must first sacrifice blood. Their lust for blood is the craving or impulse of the unconscious contents to break into consciousness. If they are denied they begin to drain energy from consciousness, leaving the individual fatigued and listless. This story indicates an attempt on the part of unconscious contents to attract the attention of consciousness, to obtain recognition of their reality and their needs and to impart something to consciousness.

By getting the head, the hero integrates its knowledge and its wisdom. With it in his possession he breaks the spell which had been cast on the princess. Although she is released, she is not yet redeemed, because the symbolic head has been grasped only in a negative form. The cutting off of the head means separating this special content from its collective unconscious background by an intuitive recognition of its specific character. In this way the hero integrates a part of the meaning, but he does not get what it is in its entirety or how it is connected with the collective unconscious. In other words, while he was able to discriminate (to separate out) the essential disturbing factor behind the anima and thereby put an end to it, he could not completely realize the roots of it; he probably never suspected the presence of the god of the early Germans, Wotan. The positive aspect of the head, the deeper understanding possessed by it, could only become manifest through a process of transformation such as that which takes place later in the anima.

One's understanding of many European fairy tales is greatly increased if one taps the rich symbolic fund of alchemical texts. As comparative material this is very useful because the alchemistic speculations were an attempt to blend the natural, heathen strain with the Christian strain in collective consciousness. The one-sided spiritualization of Christianity had brought about in certain classes an estrangement from the instinct. As Jung observes in *Psychology and Alchemy,* we are Christianized in the higher levels of the psyche, but down below we are still completely pagan. While fairy tales are for the most part entirely pagan, some of them, especially those of a late date such as this one, contain symbols which one can understand only as being an attempt of the unconscious to unite again the sunken pagan tradition with the Christian field of consciousness.

One big difference between alchemical writings and fairy tales is that the alchemists not only produced symbols by projecting their unconscious into physical materials, but they also theorized about their discoveries. Their texts abound not only in symbols but in many interesting, semipsychological associations linked up with the symbols. One can use alchemical images as connecting links between the distant fairy tale images and our world of consciousness.

In alchemy some of the usual stages described in the pattern of development—which corresponds to the refining of the crude *prima materia* into gold—are the *nigredo,* the Latin word for the blackness of the material when subjected to fire; the *albedo,* the white substance which when washed becomes silver; and the *rubedo,* the red, which through further heating turns into gold.

The *albedo* signifies the individual's first clear awareness of the unconscious, with the accompanying possibility of attaining an objective attitude, and the lowering of consciousness necessary to attain such states. The *albedo* means a cool, detached attitude, a stage where things look remote and vague, as though seen in moonlight. In the *albedo,* therefore, it is said that the feminine and the moon are ruling. It also means a receptive attitude toward the unconscious. This is the ordeal of coming to terms with the anima; whereas the former stage, the *nigredo,* marks the first terrible facing of the shadow, which is torture, and should be followed by working on and differentiating one's inferior side. The alchemists call this "the hard work." With the progress of the *albedo,* the main stream is relieved. Then simple heating changes the *albedo* into the *rubedo,* which is ruled by the sun and heralds a new state of consciousness. The sun and the moon, the red slave and the white woman, are opposites which often marry, signifying the union of objective consciousness with the anima, of the masculine Logos with the feminine inner principle. With this union, more and more energy is poured by degrees into consciousness, bringing a positive connection with the world, the possibility of love and creative activity.

The image of the mountain spirit is a parallel to Saturn, who symbolizes in alchemy a dark, low, not-yet-thought-out content which must be brought up into consciousness, the severed head. Saturn is the head, the round thing, or the "destructive water" (Zosimos calls Saturn the Omega or head). This dynamic mountain spirit does not appear to be a new god himself but a priest or an acolyte devoted to a god. Behind him must lie an unanthropomorphic figure of the Self. The worship in the mountain temple is dangerous because it is hidden in the collective unconscious.

As I pointed out earlier, in northern countries Mercurius was partially identified with Wotan, as can be seen in the fairy tales. With the cutting off of alchemy and the decline of folklore, people severed the connections with the pagan gods within their unconscious. Before this happened, it was in alchemy and folklore and astrology that the pagan gods had areas where they could live. In these three fields they made their last stand.

The mountain spirit is not redeemed, only the anima. Thus the deeper problem remained unsolved, remained a seventeenth-century anticipation of the continuing presence of Wotan waiting to be roused in the German psyche.

In our tale the danger is not yet over. On the wedding night the hero must plunge the princess three times into water until she is restored to her former self. In the Norwegian version she has to wash off her troll skin in milk. In the ancient mysteries milk played a prominent part as nourishment for the newly born initiate. In the Dionysian mountain orgies, the Maenads drank milk and honey flowing freely from the earth. Milk and honey were also the food of the reborn in early Christian baptism. In an ode of Solomon milk is extolled as a symbol of the friendliness and kindliness of God. Saint Paul says that the new Christians are children drinking the milk of the new doctrine. Milk is a symbol of the beginning of a divine rebirth in man. In ancient Greek sacrifices, milk was offered to the chthonic gods and to the newly dead. In these cases milk is cathartic (cf. the many German superstitions about obstructive demons bewitching milk and turning it blue, and the many prescribed precautions against them). Hence the washing of the anima in milk means the purging of the demonic elements in her as well as the purging of her link with death.

Skins of animals and of trolls are evidence of an unredeemed nature. In alchemy the anima may wear dirty clothes and, in alchemical parlance, be "the dove hidden in the lead." Then again, the washing or scouring off is often not done at the right time. This means that psychological contents which are insufficiently developed when the washing off takes place turn up in an unpleasant guise. Then positive drives contained in unconscious contents go unrealized and are not only disguised but pollute the instincts, materializing in ugly impulses; man's spiritual aspirations express themselves in a craving for drink, for example. Indeed, most neurotic symptoms are like troll skins covering up important positive contents of the unconscious.

In the German version, the anima emerged from the first dunking as a raven, from the second as a dove, so she evidently has the flighty element in her. Because she represents an uncontrollable, capricious, evasive content, she often appears in fairy tales as a bird.

In the Christian world, the raven was thought to be a representation of the sinner and also of the devil.[42] In antiquity, on the other hand, the raven belonged to the sun god Apollo, and in alchemy it symbolizes the *nigredo* and melancholy thoughts. The old man in the mountain who is accompanied by a raven is a frequent character in fairy tales.

The dove, on the other hand, is the bird of Venus. In the Gospel of John it represents the Holy Ghost, and in alchemy it stands for the *albedo*. The two aspects of the anima must be distinguished, her bird nature belonging to the other world and her woman side related to this world. The flighty, elusive bird nature must be released or separated out by being bathed.

The bathing is a sort of baptism, a transformation through the medium of the unconscious. This happens practically by the hero's pushing the anima back into the unconscious, which means having a critical attitude toward what is awakened and emerging into consciousness. Such an attitude is necessary because the anima and the reactions she induces in a man, although apparently human, are often deceptive. For this reason a man must always question an anima inspiration—"Is that my own real feeling?"—for the feeling of a man can be really lyrical and can soar like a lark in flight, or it can be bloodthirsty and hawklike, scarcely human—a mood or atmosphere unrelated to the human state. The milk bath of the Norwegian tale serves the same purpose—that of purifying and taking the curse out of the anima; it is an act of discrimination.

The spiritual companion's final concern is with this process of the cleansing of the anima. When her marriage to the hero is consummated, the comrade vanishes and becomes entirely spiritual. He really represents more than a shadow figure: he is an inspiring, creative spirit. But he can be this effectively only when the anima loses her demonic qualities. Only then can he come into his own.

With the fulfillment of the marriage of the hero and his anima, the task of the shadow is accomplished, as it was in "Prince Ring." Dealing with the shadow is therefore not the primary goal here;

rather, it is the finding of the genuine inner goal through which the fight between good and evil no longer holds center stage.

The Female Shadow

Not many fairy tales tell about the heroine and her shadow. The usual pattern is the banal tale of the good and bad sisters, the one loaded with rewards and the other dreadfully punished. Another possibility is the one about the girl who is banished by her stepmother and neglected and made to do the most menial housework. (These two figures lend themselves equally well to interpretation from the masculine standpoint as the two aspects of the anima.) The female shadow appears rarely in fairy tales because real women are not very sharply separated from their shadows. Such a separation in a woman is usually an animus effect, nature and instinct being more closely interwoven than in men. The female psyche displays a pendulum-like tendency to swing over from ego to shadow, as the moon moves from new to full and back to new again. There is one tale, however, which seems to be a representative example of the feminine shadow problem. Here, as is frequent in fairy tales, the problem of the shadow is intertwined with that of the animus.

Shaggy Top

A king and queen who had no children of their own adopted a little girl. One day when she was playing with her golden ball, it attracted a beggar-girl and her mother. The king and queen wished to chase them away, but the beggar-child said that her mother knew of a way to make the queen fruitful. After being coaxed with wine, the old beggar-woman told the queen that she must bathe in two vessels before retiring and then throw the water under the bed; then in the morning she would see two flowers in bloom under her bed, one fair and one foul; she was to eat the fair flower only.

In the morning when the queen tasted the fair bright flower, it was so delicious that she could not resist eating the black and ugly one as well. When her time came, her little daughter was gray and ugly and came riding to her on a he-goat. In her hand she held a wooden mixing ladle, and she was able to speak from the very first. An exquisitely fair younger daughter followed. The ugly one was called Shaggy Top because her head and part of her face were covered with shaggy tufts. She became a close friend to her younger sister.

One Christmas Eve, the noise of troll-women holding a festival reached them, and Shaggy Top went out with her ladle to chase them away. The fair princess looked out of the door, and a troll-wife snatched her head off and gave her a calf's head instead.

Shaggy Top took her unlucky sister on a ship to the land of the troll-women, found her head under a window, and made off with it. With the troll-wives after her, she raced back to the ship and changed the heads back again.

They landed in a region ruled by a king who was a widower with an only son. This king wished to marry the fair princess, but Shaggy Top made it a condition that the prince should marry her, so the king arranged for the double wedding in spite of the prince's protests about having to marry Shaggy Top.

On the wedding day, Shaggy Top told the prince to ask her why she rode such an ungainly buck. When he did so, she replied that it was indeed a beautiful horse, and the buck thereupon changed into a beautiful horse. In a similar way, the ladle became a silver fan, her shaggy cap became a golden crown, and she herself assumed a beauty even more radiant than her sister's. The wedding ceremony proved a happier event than anyone could ever have expected.[43]

The assimilation of the upper and the lower here is the same as in "Prince Ring." Again the shadow is redeemed by being made conscious, and it seems possible to conclude that for man and woman the shadow really boils down to the same problem.

The motif of the childless king and queen is generally a forerunner of the miraculous birth of a very distinguished child. In itself the childlessness testifies that the connection with the creative earth of the psyche has been broken and that a gulf lies between the values and ideas of collective consciousness and the dark, fertile loam of unconscious, archetypal processes of transformation.

We may regard the two leading figures, the fair princess and Shaggy Top, as parallels to Ring and Snati-Snati. We took Ring to be an impulse in the collective unconscious that was tending to build up a new form of consciousness. Shaggy Top, however, may represent an impulse to restore the feeling connection with the depths of the unconscious and with nature, since in life it is the task of women to renew feeling values.

Before the birth of these two children the queen does her best to remedy the situation by adopting a girl. This very positive decision evokes—like magic by analogy—a fertilizing reaction in the matrix of the unconscious. By means of the golden ball, which may be taken as a symbol of the Self, the adopted child attracts a poor child and her mother. The function of the Self-symbol is to unite the dark and the light aspects of the psyche, and in this case Mother Nature is constellated: the beggar-woman personifies the instinctive knowledge that belongs to nature.

She gives clear advice to the queen to throw the water in which she has washed under the bed and to eat one of the flowers which will grow in it. To keep the dirty water within the bedroom probably means that the queen should not cast out her own dark side but should accept it within her most intimate surroundings, because in this dirty water—her shadow—lies also her own fertility. This seems to be the age-old maternal secret of the old woman.

The bright flower and the dark flower anticipate the opposite natures of the two daughters. They signify their as yet unborn souls and they also symbolize feeling. By eating both flowers instead of just one, the queen reveals an urge to integrate the totality, not only the brighter aspect of the unconscious, and by so doing, she also commits the sin of disobedience—a *beata culpa* (a fortunate guilt)—which brings forth new trouble but with it a higher realization. This is similar to the motif where Ring opens the door of the forbidden kitchen and finds Snati-Snati.

Shaggy Top as the shadow of the new form of life has all the exuberance and initiative that is lacking in consciousness. That she grows up so rapidly points to her demonic qualities and spiritlike nature, while the he-goat on which she rides is the animal of Thor and suggests that the essence of Shaggy Top belongs to the chthonic and pagan world. The ladle characterizes her as witchlike, one who has always got something cooking, who stirs up a welter of emotions in order to bring them to the boil. The fur cap she wears is the sign of the animal traits in her and also can be a symbol of animus possession. In certain tales, the heroine puts on shaggy headgear when she is persecuted by her father, and this act indicates a regression into the animal domain because of the animus problem. It therefore looks as if an animal-like unconsciousness clings to Shaggy Top, which implies a possession by animal impulses and emotions. This, however, is only an outer appearance, just as it was with Snati-Snati.

In northern countries the pagan layer of the unconscious is still very much alive, and therefore the trolls are depicted as having their midsummer festival at Christmas. When the curious princess gapes at them from the doorway, they seize her head and replace it with the head of a calf. The trolls themselves often have the tails of cows, according to northern folklore, and we may conclude from the transposition of the heads that the princess is assimilated by the trolls; she literally loses her head and becomes possessed by contents of the collective unconscious; she often appears to be completely silly, gauche, and unable to express herself. This happens because her whole feeling life has fallen under the control of dark powers of the unconscious and events are occurring in her inner world which she cannot bring out.

Shaggy Top is able to outwit the trolls and redeem her sister from this state because she shares the trolls' nature to a certain extent. Just as Snati-Snati knew better than Ring how to overcome the giants, so Shaggy Top is more than a match for the trolls.

After Shaggy Top redeems her sister, the story takes an unexpected turn, and instead of sailing for home they continue their journey into a strange kingdom where there are no women, only a widower king and a prince. Since the first court had several women and a barren king, in the second kingdom we find the elements which make up for what was lacking in the first. The two realms are like two compensatory parts of the psyche; incomplete in themselves, they form a totality when put together. It is natural, therefore, that when the king proposes to marry the princess, Shaggy Top should demand the hand of the prince. The double marriage constitutes what Jung calls a marriage quaternity, a four-square symbol of the Self.[44]

Shaggy Top gets redeemed herself not only by assisting at her sister's wedding (like Snati-Snati again) but by certain questions she induces the prince to ask. This recalls the Parsival saga in which Parsival at first fails to ask the redeeming question, consciousness being still too juvenile to be aware of what is growing in the unconscious toward the light. Shaggy Top is the strong, dynamic factor in the unconscious which compels consciousness to realize that which strives to be realized. Here we have a beautiful example of unconscious nature itself endeavoring to equip the human being to reach a new, higher level of consciousness. The impulse often has its starting point in the source of the shadow and is gradually and fully humanized.

The general structure of this fairy tale is interesting in its placing of the quaternary systems. We have two groups of four persons. First the king and queen, their adopted child, and her poor friend, whose relations are not harmonious. The helpful intervention of the beggar-woman brings about the coming of the second pair of girls, Shaggy Top and the fair princess, who replace the former children. The disturbing interference of the trolls indicates that this quaternity is still too artificial and too detached from the deep unconscious. When the princess and Shaggy Top marry the king and the prince, they merge into a new quaternity. This new group seems to be a model representation of the Self, like the group of four persons at the close of "Prince Ring." Here again, the tale opens with a symbol of the Self and culminates in a symbol of the Self, thus representing eternal processes within this nucleus of the collective psyche.

THE POWER OF THE ANIMUS

The animus is perhaps less well known in literature than the anima, but in folklore we find many very impressive representations of this archetype. Fairy tales also present patterns that show how a woman can deal with this inner figure in contrast to the man's way of dealing with the anima. This is not merely a simple reversal. Every step in becoming conscious of the animus is differently characterized. The following tale is a good example of this.

King Thrushbeard

A king has a beautiful daughter who mocks all her suitors and will accept no one. One suitor with a pointed chin she mockingly dubs Thrushbeard, with the result that he is known thereafter as King Thrushbeard. Exasperated, the old king declares that he will give her to the first beggar who comes near the court, and he fulfills his threat by wishing her off on a poor fiddler who appears in court and who attracts the king's attention with his music. [In a variation, the attraction is a golden spinning-wheel.]

The princess becomes the fiddler's wife, but she is incapable of doing housework, and her husband is dissatisfied with her. He makes her cook, then weave baskets and spin, all of which tasks she fails at. Then finally she has to sell pottery at the market. One morning a drunken hussar rides over the vessels, and her husband scolds her for the loss. He tells her that she is good for nothing and sends her to the king's court nearby to be a kitchen-maid.

One night she furtively watches the dance at the wedding of the prince at that court. The servants throw morsels of food to her, which she hides in her pockets. When she is seen by the prince, who invites her to dance, she blushes and tries to escape and spills the food. He catches her and reveals that he is King Thrushbeard and that it is he who has been masquerading as her beggar-husband, and also as the hussar, in order to break her pride.[45]

The name Thrushbeard has affinities with Bluebeard, but Bluebeard is a murderer and nothing more; he cannot transform his wives or be transformed himself. He embodies the deathlike, ferocious aspects of the animus in his most diabolical form; from him only flight is possible. Animi in this guise are often met with in mythology (for example in "Fitcher's Bird" and "The Robber Bridegroom").

This throws into bold relief an important difference between the anima and the animus. Man in his primitive capacity as hunter and warrior is accustomed to kill, and it as if the animus, being masculine, shares this propensity. Woman, on the other hand, serves life, and the anima entangles a man in life. In tales that feature the anima, her completely deadly aspect does not often appear; rather, she is the archetype of life for the man.

The animus in his negative form seems to be the opposite. He draws woman away from life and murders life for her. He has to do with ghostlands and the land of death. Indeed, he may appear as the personification of death itself, as in the French tale called "The Wife of Death," which goes as follows:

> A woman rejects all her suitors but accepts Death when he appears. While he is out on his job, she lives in his castle. Her brother comes to see the gardens of Death and they walk about together. Then the brother rescues the girl, taking her back to life, and she discovers that she has been away for five thousand years.[46]

A Gypsy variation with the same title goes like this:

> An unknown traveler arrives at the remote hut of a solitary girl. He receives food and lodging for a few days and falls in love with her. They marry, and she dreams that he is white and cold, that he is the King of the Dead. He is then compelled to leave her and resume his mournful trade. When finally he reveals to her that he is Death, she dies from the shock.[47]

The negative animus often gives one the feeling of being separated from life. One feels tortured and unable to go on living. This is the disastrous effect of the animus on a woman. He cuts her off from participation in life.

In his attempt to sever the woman's connections with the outside world, the animus may take on the aspect of a father. In "Thrushbeard" there is only a king and his daughter, and the princess's inaccessibility and refusal of all suitors is evidently related to the fact that she lives alone with her father. Her scornful, mocking, critical attitude toward the suitors is typical of a woman ruled by the animus. Such an attitude tears all relationships to shreds.

It is ostensibly the arrogance of the daughter that provokes the exasperation of the father, but actually a father frequently binds his daughter to him and puts obstacles in the path of prospective suitors. If we discern this attitude in the background, we recognize the typical ambivalence of parents who hold their children back from life and at the same time have no patience with them for being unable to escape into life. (Mothers are frequently the same way with their sons.) In retaliation, the father complex working in the daughter seeks to wound a powerful father by causing the girl to take on inferior lovers.

In another tale, the animus appears first as an old man who later turns into a youth, which is a way of saying that the old man—the father image—is only a temporary aspect of the animus and that behind this mask is a young man.

A more vivid example of the isolating effect of the animus is to be found in a Siberian tale in which the father actually locks the beautiful daughter in a stone chest. Then a poor youth rescues her and they escape together. In a tale from Turkestan, "The Magic Horse," the father sells his daughter outright to a Div, an evil spirit, in return for the answer to a riddle.[48] In the Balkan tale "The Girl and the Vampire," a youth who is actually a vampire abducts a girl and puts her into a grave in a cemetery.[49] She flees underground into a wood and prays to God for a box that she can hide in. To be hidden, the girl has to suffer being sealed in, in order to protect herself against the animus.

The threatening action of the animus and the woman's defensive reaction against it always go hand in glove and bring to mind the double aspect of all animus activity. The animus can either lame one or make one very aggressive. Women either become masculine and assertive or they tend to be absent-minded, as if they are not fully present—perhaps charmingly feminine but as if partly asleep—and the fact is that such women have marvelous journeys with the animus-lover; they enter into a kind of submerged day-dreaming with the animus, of which they are not fully aware.

To return to the Siberian story, a prince discovers the box with the girl inside, frees her, and they marry. The box and the stone chest are representations of the state of being cut off from life, which is endured by the animus-possessed woman. Contrary to this, if one has an aggressive animus and tries to act spontaneously, it is always the animus that does the acting. Some women, however, refuse to be aggressive and difficult, and so they cannot let him out. They cannot see how to handle the animus, and in order to keep him off, they are stiff and conventionally correct and frozen, imprisoned in themselves. This also is a lameness, but it comes from the woman's reaction toward the animus. In a Norwegian tale, a woman is compelled to wear a wooden coat. Such a cumbersome covering, made of tough living tissue, illustrates the stiffness toward the world and the burden such a defensive armor becomes. The motif of escaping into a trap, as in the episode of the seaside-witch throwing Ring into the cask, is at once an act of bewitchment and protection. Historically, the animus, like the anima, has a pre-Christian form. Thrushbeard (*Drosselbart*) is a name for Wotan, the same as *Rossbart*—"Horsebeard."

The stalemate in "Thrushbeard" is broken up by the father's exasperation, which causes him to give his daughter away to a poor man. In parallel tales she is beguiled by the beggar's beautiful singing, and in a Nordic parallel the beggar enchants her with a golden spinning wheel. In other words, the animus has a fascinating attraction for her.

The spinning activity has to do with wishful thinking. Wotan is the lord of wishes and the typical spirit of such magic thought. "The wish turns the wheels of thought." Both the spinning wheel and the act of spinning are proper to Wotan, and in our tale the girl has to spin to support her husband. The animus has thus taken possession of her own properly feminine activity. A danger implicit in the animus preempting a feminine activity is that it leads to a loss of any real thinking on the part of the woman. It brings about a lassitude, so that instead of thinking she lazily spins daydreams and unwinds wishful fantasies, or else she spins plots and intrigues. The king's daughter in "Thrushbeard" has fallen into such an unconscious activity.

Another role of the animus is that of the poor servant. His unexpected gallantry in this guise is revealed in a Siberian tale.

> A woman lives alone except for her servant. Her father has died, and the servant becomes unmanageable. However, he consents to kill a bear to make a coat for her. After he accomplishes that, she bids him perform ever harder tasks, and each time he rises to the occasion. It turns out that though he seems poor, he is really wealthy.

The animus appears to be poor and often never reveals the great treasures of the unconscious which are at his disposal. In the role of a poor man or a beggar, he induces the woman to believe that she herself has nothing. This is the penalty for a prejudice against the unconscious—a lasting poverty in conscious life, resulting in endless criticism and self-criticism.

After the fiddler marries the princess, he points out to her the wealth of Thrushbeard, and she greatly regrets having refused him. It is typical for an animus-ridden woman to suffer remorse about something she has failed to do. Lamenting over what might have been is a pseudo-feeling of guilt and is completely sterile. One sinks into the despairing feeling of having utterly ruined one's prospects and having missed life altogether.

At first the princess is incapable of doing the housework, and this is another symptom of the touch of the animus—listlessness, inertia, and a glassy, staring expression. This may sometimes look like feminine passivity, but a woman in this trancelike state is not receptive; she is drugged by animus-inertia and imprisoned in a stone chest.

Living in a hovel, the princess must do the house chores and make baskets for money, which humiliates her and increases her feeling of inferiority. As a compensation for high-flown ambitions, the animus often forces a woman into a way of life far below her real capacity. If she is unable to adjust to what does not coincide with her lofty ideals, then she does lowly work in pure despair. This is thinking in extremes: "If I cannot marry a god, then I'll marry a lousy beggar." At the same time, a boundless pride persists, nourished by a secret fantasy life in which one dreams passionately of immense fame and glory. Humility and arrogance are intertwined.

This lowly activity is also a kind of compensation to persuade the woman to become feminine again. The effect of animus pressure can lead a woman to deeper femininity, providing she accepts the fact that she is animus-possessed and does something to bring her animus into reality. If she gives him a field of action—that is, if she takes up some special study or does some masculine work—this can occupy the animus, and at the same time her feeling will be vivified and she will come back to feminine activities. The worst condition comes about when a woman has a powerful animus and does not even live it; then she is straightjacketed by animus opinions, and while she may avoid any sort of work that seems in the least masculine, she is much less feminine.

Because the princess bungles all her tasks, her husband sends her out to sell earthen pots in the market. Vessels are feminine symbols, and she is driven to sell her femininity at a low price—too cheaply and too collectively. The more animus-possessed a woman is, the more she feels estranged from men and the more painful are her efforts to make a good feeling contact. Although she may compensate by taking the lead in erotic affairs, there can be no genuine love or passion in them. If she really had a good contact with men, she would have no need to be so assertive. She acts out of the vague realization that something is wrong and makes desperate attempts to make up for what has been lost because of her animus-imposed estrangement from men. This is merely walking blindly into a new catastrophe. A new animus attack is bound to follow, and in the story it does: a drunken hussar breaks all her vessels to pieces. This symbolizes a brutal outburst of emotion. The wild, ungovernable animus smashes everything, showing clearly that such an exhibition of her unconscious nature does not work.

The life with the beggar-husband also brings about the final humiliation, and this occurs when the girl peeps through the door to glimpse the splendor of the court world and Thrushbeard's wedding party. Peeping through a crack in the door is interpreted in the *I Ching* as having too narrow and too subjective a standpoint. Hampered by this, one is unable to see what one really has. The inferiority of a woman who thinks she must admire others and nurses secret jealousy toward them means being unable to assess one's own real worth.

From hunger, she accepts scraps of food thrown to her by the servants, and then to her intense shame, her greed and inferiority are exposed when the food falls to the floor. She wants to get life on any terms and assumes that she cannot get it in her own right. A king's daughter accepting scraps thrown by servants? That is going below one's scorn. Then she feels ashamed and despises herself, but this humiliation is what is needed, for, as we see in the story, the heroine then realizes that she is after all the daughter of a king. Only then does she learn that Thrushbeard is in fact her husband.

In this story the animus—as Thrushbeard, as the wild hussar, and as the beggar-husband—assumes three roles that the god Wotan is known to effect. It is said of him that he is the man riding a white horse who leads the wild riders of the night, who sometimes carry their heads in their arms. This legend, which still lingers, comes from the early idea of Wotan as the leader of the dead warriors going to Valhalla. As evil ghosts they still hunt in the woods, and it is death to look at them, death to be swept into their ranks.

Often Wotan goes about as a beggar, an unknown wanderer in the night, and always his face is partly concealed, for he has only one eye. A stranger enters, says a few words, and leaves—and afterward one realizes that it was Wotan. He calls himself the owner of the land, and psychically this is true: the unknown owner of the land is still the archetypal Wotan.[50]

The name Wotan brings up another of his attributes: his theriomorphic form is the horse. His horse is Sleipnir, the eight-legged white or black horse, swift as the wind. This indicates that while the animus is mostly a sort of archaic divine spirit, he is also connected with our instinctive animal nature. In the unconscious, spirit and instinct are not opposites. On the contrary, new spiritual germs often manifest themselves first in an uprush of sexual libido or instinctive impulses and only later develop their other aspect. This is because they are generated by the spirit of nature, by the meaningfulness inherent in our instinctive pattern. In women the spirit has not yet become differentiated and retains its archaic emotional and instinctive characteristics, which is why women usually get excited when they do any genuine thinking.

The animal aspect of the animus shows up in "Beauty and the Beast," but this motif is relatively rare in fairy tales. A less well-known example is the story from Turkestan, "The Magic Horse."

A girl takes a magic horse and flees from her captor, a Div, a desert-demon. She escapes temporarily but is overtaken by the demon. Finally the horse plunges with the Div into the sea, and the Div is overcome. The horse then commands the girl to kill him. When she does so, he changes into a heavenly palace, and his four legs become the pillars of the four corners. Finally the heroine is reunited with her real lover, a young prince.

Here the animus is an evil spirit on the one side and a helpful animal on the other. When the animus takes the form of an entirely destructive and diabolical spirit, the instincts must come to the rescue.

One way of dealing with the animus problem is for the woman simply to suffer it through to the bitter end. Indeed, there is no solution that does not include suffering, and suffering seems to belong to the life of woman.

In cases where a woman has to escape a state of possession by some ghost or vampire, much can be gained by an extreme passivity toward the animus, and often the wisest counsel is that she should do nothing now. There are times when one can only wait and try to fortify oneself by keeping the positive aspects of the animus in mind. To overcome possession by an unconscious content by slipping out of its grasp is as meritorious as a heroic victory. This is the motif of the "magic flight," which symbolizes a situation where it is better to flee from the unconscious than to seek to overcome it, and by so doing avoid being devoured.

The motif of the magic flight is prominent in a Siberian tale, "The Girl and the Evil Spirit."[51] The heroine, who knew no man and could not say who her parents were, is a herdswoman of reindeer. She wanders about, keeping her reindeer by singing magic songs to them.

Here again the motif of loneliness occurs as a prodromal symptom of a special individual development of the personality. It is a situation in which a flood of inner images can rise up from the unconscious and bring about unexpected reactions. This girl is not destitute or hungry; she can cook and care for herself, and she can keep her reindeer with her by the magic charm of her singing. In other words, she is resourceful, more gifted and more normal than the girl in the foregoing tale, and her magic gifts signify that she has the ability to express the contents of the unconscious. (In analysis, one sometimes sees that a situation is dangerous because the patient's way of conceiving and expressing the turbulent, threatening contents of the unconscious is too feeble and too narrow. This may be a poverty of heart and a failure to give love as well as a barrenness of mind and spirit; the old bottles are unable to contain the new wine.) The songs on the lips of the girl probably come from her traditional past, and this would mean that a fortunate constellation of ancestral units has been inherited by her. But she is without human connections. Being cut off from society is a great danger for a woman because without human contact she easily becomes unconscious and surrenders to the grip of the negative animus.

The tale goes on to relate that suddenly a tremendous pair of jaws comes down from heaven—an open abyss stretching from heaven to earth. This gaping, devouring mouth is the abyss of complete unconsciousness. The girl hurls her staff onto the ground behind her.

The staff is a sign of power and of judgment, two royal prerogatives symbolized by the king's scepter. The staff is also associated with the Way and is a direction-giving principle in the unconscious. The bishop's staff, for instance, was interpreted by the church as the authority of the doctrine, which shows the way and gives decisions. Thus in a woman the staff is a form of the animus. In antiquity, the golden staff or magic rod belonged to Mercurius and represents his ability to marshal intractable elements within the unconscious. If one has a staff, one is not wholly passive; one has a direction.

The girl runs, throwing her magic comb and her red handkerchief behind her. Bestrewing one's trail with objects is characteristic of the magic flight. This act of throwing away things of value is a sacrifice; one throws things over one's shoulder to the dead, or to spirits, or to the devil, to propitiate those whom we dare not face. It may seem panicky to abandon valuable possessions when one is escaping, but one who stiffens himself into a defensive attitude is easily cut down by an assailant stronger than himself, whereas stripping oneself gives mobility. There are situations in which one absolutely has to give up wanting anything, and in this way one slips out from under; one is not there any longer, so nothing more can go wrong. When one is confronted by a hopelessly wrong situation, one must just make a drastic leap to the bottom of open-minded simplicity, and from there one can live through it.

What is more, the objects which have been sacrificed generally transform themselves into obstacles for the pursuer. The comb at once turns into a forest and becomes a part of nature—the hair of Mother Earth. Its transformation into a natural object suggests that originally it was an integral part of nature. Actually, there is no thought or instrument or object that has not originated from nature; that is, from the unconscious psyche. One sacrifices to the unconscious what once was wrested from it.

The comb is used to arrange and confine the hair. Hair is a source of magic power or mana. Ringlets of hair, preserved as keepsakes, are believed to connect one individual with another over a distance. Cutting the hair and sacrificing it often means submission to a new collective state—a giving up and a rebirth. The coiffure is frequently an expression of a cultural *Weltanschauung.* Primitive folk tales speak of demons being deloused and combed when they are caught, which means that the confusion in the unconscious has to be straightened out, ordered, and made conscious. Because of this meaning, hair in wild disarray is often dreamed of at the start of an analysis. The comb, therefore, represents a capacity for making one's thoughts ordered, clear, and conscious.

The red handkerchief that the girl gives up becomes a flame soaring from earth to heaven. To abandon the staff and comb meant not attempting to marshal herself or to think out a plan. Now the flame indicates that she puts an inner distance between herself and her feelings and emotions. She is reduced to a passive simplicity.

In the tale, the gaping jaws devour the forest and spit water on the flame. Water and fire battle in the unconscious, and in the meantime the girl escapes between the opposites.

Then she goes through four animal transformations, each succeeding animal being fleeter of foot than the preceding one. Now she can only rely on her inner animal side. She must relinquish all higher activities and burrow down into the instinctive level. There are moments of imminent danger when one must not think or even feel or try to escape by struggling but must go down into an animal simplicity. Supported by a purposeful attitude, this Oriental "doing nothing" succeeds where strong resistance would incur failure. The ego escapes and vanishes. And that is all the human being can do at certain times. Then the persecuting demon is left to eat up the forest and combat the flame.

The girl changes into a bear with copper bells in his ears. Bells and similar-sounding instruments are used to drive away evil spirits. (Churchbells originally had this purpose.) They also announce a decisive moment, like the roll of a drum or of thunder, and induce a psychic resonance in the emotions of the hearer so that he feels that the decisive event is about to happen—for example, the triple bell in the Mass. Bells in the girl's animal-ears exclude all other sounds, sounds that she must not listen to because their effect is poisonous, words that the negative animus whispers to her. The poisoning occurs when one accepts them and takes on convictions and ways of behaving which do not suit one. The vessel that conveys this poisonous influence is the ear, and the bells are a defense against noxious animus effects.

The tale ends with the girl falling to earth in a dead faint before a white tent, and suddenly the evil spirit stands before her as a beautiful man. She has fled from him to him. Her perseverance in the one instinctively right course has brought about the enantiodromia, with the result that the menacing demon has transformed itself into a gracious young man. In fact, his secret intention had been to bring her here to his white tent. He has three younger brothers, and from the four she may choose whom she will have for her husband. Her inner balance and her totality are expressed in these four figures. Three equal figures almost always signify a fateful constellation: the three dimensions of space and the three aspects of time—past, present, and future—are vessels of fate. Here the three brothers may be the three inferior functions of the girl; the three-plus-one, the four, portends individuation. The girl chooses the eldest because she recognizes that the realization of her fate lies in accepting the spirit who persecuted her.

When an individual with a developed consciousness feels the promise of meaningful activity stored in the animus, it is futile to take flight or to try to test its meaning intellectually. Instead, one should use the energy provided by the animus in a suitable way by undertaking some masculine activity such as intellectual creative work; otherwise, one is dominated and possessed. Similarly, a powerful mother complex cannot be subdued by the intellect alone. A tragic state of possession can be a fateful summons to commit oneself to the process of individuation. When the father or mother complex is recognized as being stronger than the ego, it can then be accepted as a component of one's individuality.

Another ordeal of an animus-ridden woman is presented in the following tale.

The Woman Who Married the Moon and the Kele

A woman, abandoned by her husband, was so faint with hunger that she could only crawl on all fours. Twice she went to the house of the Moon-man and ate the food that she found on a plate. The third time he grabbed her as she was eating, and when he learned that she had no husband, married her.

Each day their food appeared by magic upon the empty plate. When the Moon-man went out, he forbade the wife to open a certain chest and look inside, but the lure proved irresistible and she discovered in the chest a strange woman whose face was half red and half black. It was she who had been secretly supplying them with food, but she now died when exposed to the air. When the Moon-man returned he discovered that his wife had disobeyed him and was very angry. He restored the dead woman to life and took his wife back to her father, saying that he could not control her and that her former husband must have had good reason to abandon her.

Angered by the daughter's return, the father invoked an evil spirit to marry her. This demon, the Kele, ate men, even the woman's own brother, whose corpse he brought her to eat. Acting upon the advice of a little fox, however, she made shoes for the Kele. When she threw them in front of him, a spider-thread descended from above upon which she could climb up to the house of the spider woman. Pursued by the Kele, she continued to climb until she reached the immovable one, the North Star, which is the creator and the highest god. The Kele, who also had arrived there, was imprisoned in a chest by the protective Polar Star. He almost died and was released only on condition that he would no longer persecute the woman.

She returned to earth and made her father sacrifice reindeer to the god. Suddenly the father and then the daughter died. (This colourless, anti-climatic ending is typical of primitive stories.)[52]

The protagonist is a woman abandoned by her husband, and afterwards the Moon-man declares that the husband certainly must have had reason to abandon her. Loneliness, poverty, and hunger are stressed, typical states that result from animus-possession. A woman's attitude largely conditions the events that befall her.

The animus fosters loneliness in women, whereas the anima thrusts men headlong into relationships and the confusion that accompanies them. The hunger is also typical. Woman needs life, relationships with people, and participation in meaningful activity. Part of her hunger comes from an awareness of dormant, unused aptitudes. The animus contributes to her unrest so that she is never satisfied; one must always do more for an animus-possessed woman. Not realizing that the problem is an inner one, such women assume that if only they can go about more, spend more money and surround themselves with more friends, their life-hunger will be assuaged.

The moon god often appears as the mysterious, invisible lover of a married woman in fairy tales. The moon is sometimes represented in mythology and in dreams as a man, sometimes as a woman, and at other times as a hermaphroditic being. Perhaps we can identify what determines the moon's gender.

The moon is closely related to the sun, but it is a lesser light, owing its light to the sun. The sun is really a divinity—the source of consciousness within the unconscious—and represents an active psychic factor that can create greater awareness. The moon, however, symbolizes a primitive, softer, more diffused consciousness—a dim awareness. When the sun is feminine, as in the German language, it means that the source of consciousness is still in the unconscious, that there is no mature consciousness but a penumbral consciousness with a welter of detail not clearly distinguished. The instinct for architectural achievement among the Balinese illustrates this condition: in Bali various craftsmen set to work at their own special building skills, undirected by any plan or architect but guided from within exactly as if they had a blueprint to follow. When the various parts of the building are assembled, they fit exactly and perfectly, although each has been made individually. In this way a temple of harmonious design is created. Like the sun lighting up the unconscious, an unconscious principle of order apparently operates within the Balinese craftsman.

The moon illustrates the same principle as the sun, but it is less concentrated, less intense; it is a light of consciousness but a milder light. (The principle of consciousness operating within the woman in the story is very indefinite. This connects with her state of animus-possession, since it is characteristic of the animus to be indefinite in his overall and long-term purposes, although he is sharply insistent when it comes to details.) In mythology, the moon is associated with snakes, nocturnal animals, spirits of the dead, and gods of the underworld. In alchemy, it is called "the child of Saturn." To Paracelsus the moon was a source of poison, like the eyes of women when the moon is troubling their blood. He believed that the moon is a spirit which can renew itself and become a child again, and for this reason it is susceptible to a woman's evil eye. In this way the sidereal spirit is poisoned and then casts its baneful spell upon men who gaze at it. We may psychologically interpret Paracelsus as saying that poisonous opinions emanating from the animus can go directly into the unconscious of others with the result that people seem to have been poisoned by an undefined source. Such opinions infect the air and blight the surroundings, and one breathes them in unsuspectingly. Animus convictions sink in more deeply than a merely wrong opinion and are far more difficult to spot and throw off.

The moon divinity in this tale is ambiguous; he is concealing a woman in a chest, a dark feminine side of nature. She is undeveloped, secret, buried, but also important in that she is living and is the provider of nourishment; in other words, she is a preform or a precursor of the Self. Here she stands behind the animus (the

Moon-man) as a supporting figure. The mountain spirit was also a hidden vessel of energy standing behind the princess-anima, but he was a malevolent figure, whereas the woman in the box is a rather dim fertility goddess.

By disobeying the Moon-man and opening the chest, the heroine unwittingly kills the dark woman. Now, the transgression for which an innocent victim pays with his life is a variation of the theme of premature enlightenment, a motif that occurs in the antique tales of Eros and Psyche and of Orpheus and Eurydice, as well as in the Grimms' "The Singing, Soaring Lion's Lark." The point of this is that for everything there is a season; possession often produces systematic tactlessness in a woman. Where there are any signs of life, she cannot resist poking around, and all that should remain in the dim background of consciousness—all that needs darkness in which to grow—is hauled up into the light and lost. Mothers of this disposition tend to drag out all their children's secrets so that spontaneity and the possibility of growth are blighted. Such an interfering attitude has an unwholesome effect on the entire environment.

The woman in the tale, having been abandoned and having lost her feminine feeling, is driven by curiosity to break into the background of the Moon-man's secrets. Wild curiosity is an expression of a sort of primitive masculinity in a woman. When possessed by such a hounding, inquisitive spirit, she does the wrong things and is always at fault.

The Moon-man sends the woman back to her father. Although the father was not spoken of earlier in the story, we may suppose that he has sown the seeds of the unhappy ending. That both father and daughter die simultaneously at the end shows how close their relationship is. After the woman is sent back to her father, it is his curse that condemns her to live with an evil spirit. According to primitive belief, an expressed wish such as this can shape unborn events and bring them forth out of the womb of time. The curse condemning the daughter to live with an evil spirit is a clear indication that the father fosters the animus's domination of his daughter.

The evil spirit Kele is a body eater, a typical practice of the negative animus. Just as vampires drink blood, spirits consume bodies in order to become visible; they seize and feast upon a corpse to gain substance in that form. Thus spirits are bewitched into corpses. Vampires, as is well known, feed upon living people. Their urge to live on the lives of others comes from their desperation at being banished from the world of the living. An animus-possessed woman battens on the lives of those in her surroundings because her own sources of feeling and of Eros are withheld from her. Viewed psychologically, spirits are contents of the unconscious. The devouring of corpses shows symbolically that complexes and other unconscious contents strive desperately to enter consciousness and to be realized in living people. The ravenous hunger of a spirit for a body is an unrecognized, unredeemed wish for the fullness of life.

In contrast to this, the red and black woman in the hidden chest bestows magic food and is life-giving. Yet the other woman cannot accept her because she cannot coordinate the dark woman and the Moon-god; she cannot deal with the undeveloped figure of the Self and also become more feminine. Between the protecting Polar Star and the evil, body-devouring Kele there is a similar breach. Both are divine principles engaged in eternal warfare.

Like the woman in "The Magic Horse," mentioned above, she makes good her escape from the evil spirit with the help of an animal. By putting spirit and nature into an intolerable opposition, the animus may draw a woman into a split situation. When this happens she has to trust her instinct. In this case, her instinctive nature is represented by a fox. In China and Japan the fox is a witch-animal. Witches are wont to appear in the form of foxes. Cases of hysterical and epileptic women are explained as bewitchment by foxes. To the Chinese and Japanese the fox is as much a feminine animal as the cat is to us, and it also represents the primitive, instinctive feminine nature of woman.

The fox in the story counsels the woman to throw the shoes at the Kele to retard him while she climbs up the spider's thread to heaven.[53] The shoe is a symbol of power, for which reason we speak of being "under someone's heel" or "stepping into one's father's shoes." Clothing may represent either the persona, our outer attitude, or an inner attitude, and the changing of clothes in the mysteries stood for transformation into an enlightened understanding. Shoes are the lowest part of our clothing and represent our standpoint in relation to reality—how solidly our feet are planted on the ground; how solidly the earth supports us gives the measure of our power.

Throwing the shoe at the Kele is a gesture of propitiation that hinders him in his pursuit. It is necessary to sacrifice something in order to escape from his grasp. In this case it is the sacrifice of the old standpoint. In the clutches of the animus, no woman is able to give up whatever power she may have or her conviction that it is right and necessary and valuable. The convictions a woman has lived by spring from inferior masculine thinking; the less she herself is able to evaluate them, the more passionately she clings to them. This is a reason for the persistence of the animus possession. Unfortunately such a woman never thinks that anything could be wrong with herself and is convinced that the fault lies with others. The fox really is saying to her: "Don't become stiff. Unbend a little. Give up part of your standpoint and see what happens."

Then at once a thread from heaven gives her the means of reaching the Pole Star, which signifies the animus refined to the highest form, an image of God. (Parallel to this is Sophia, who is the highest, most spiritual form of the anima.) If one goes deeply into what the animus is, one finds that he is a divinity and that through woman's relation to him in this form, she enters into genuine religious experience. In the story, the discovery of the Pole Star is the woman's personal experience of God.

When the Kele pursues her and storms the summit, a conflict on a cosmic scale rages between him and the Pole Star so that the woman is placed between the two overwhelming world principles of good and evil—God and the Devil. When the Pole Star opens his box, light pours out, and when he closes it, snow falls on the earth. The evil spirit is flung into this box and tortured by cruel rays of light. The animus must sometimes be handled severely by a higher power.

By going to heaven, the woman has removed herself from human reality, and this affords no real solution. Anyone in this condition would be very near to borderline psychosis, swinging back and forth between exaggerated negative and positive animus possession. This tale apparently reveals the case of a weak consciousness, which is to be expected in a primitive culture. It therefore makes sense that the Pole Star says to the woman: "You had better go home; you had better get back to earth." He demands the sacrifice of two reindeer, knowing that the woman will have to make a sacrifice in order to reenter the life on earth. (There is a similar motif in Grimm's "The Golden Bird.") To come down out of the clouds of fantasy into reality is charged with danger. In this moment all one's effort and work can be lost. For example, one understands one's problem as presented in a dream, but what is one going to do about it practically? The issue is joined and the outcome awaits one's effective participation in life. The problem has been dealt with only when the latent possibilities of one's nature have been realized in creative work. The return to reality takes another form when practical problems arise that compel one to return from the adventurous quest in the unconscious. A problem also arises when one has developed an individual relationship with another and then has to face the world's disapproval and hostility. There is always the danger that one will completely reject the experiences in the unconscious and regard them cynically as nothing but this or that or, as in this story, that one becomes too dreamy and unaware of reality and tries to live out one's fantasies when a realistic adaptation is demanded.

Often in primitive tales when a satisfactory ending seems imminent, the whole thing blows up. In this one the father and daughter die and there is no dissolution of the identification between them, so the entire problem of animus-possession remains unconscious.

It is often imperative for a woman to escape from the baleful mastery of the animus. This tale tells of such an attempt, but the whole experience is known only to the unconscious. A comparable unconscious interplay is portrayed in the South American tale of the anima as a skeleton dancing in the Beyond, with the subsequent death of the hero. Early primitive tales are filled with melancholy because many primitive tribes experience the unconscious as being dismal, doleful, and frightful. It has this aspect especially for those who need above all to go into life; that is, for young people and for those who are too sheltered and secluded; the hero's escape from the unconscious is the equal in high achievement to his subsequent great deed of killing the dragon.

Another Siberian tale that illustrates the realization of the animus is "The Girl and the Skull." At the beginning of the tale a girl, living with her elderly parents, finds a skull in the wilderness and brings it home and talks to it. When the parents discover what she has done, they are horrified, decide she is a Kele, and abandon her.

That the animus appears first as a skull in this tale shows his deathlike nature. The alchemists used a skull as the vessel in which to cook the *prima materia*. According to primitive beliefs, the skull contains the immortal essence of mortal beings, and from this belief come the hunting of skulls and skull cults. For the North American Indians, the scalps they took contained the essence of the enemy. In this tale, the skull again represents the animus in his death aspect, especially in his activities that relate to the head, such as poisoning women with his noxious opinions or blinding their eyes to the treasures of the unconscious.

The parents ruefully conclude that their daughter has been changed into an evil spirit, a Kele, by marrying one and that she is beyond redemption. Their mistrustful attitude is typical of the primitive fear of being possessed by spirits, which are numerous, far-ranging, and ever-present, and thus always an imminent danger. The idea of a skull ghost has to do with the head or intellect becoming autonomous and separated from the instincts; then it can roll downhill to destruction. On the other hand, the skull is a symbol of the Self. (The aspect presented by a content of the unconscious depends on the conscious attitude with which it is viewed.)

Because they feel that the daughter is possessed, the elderly parents break up their home and travel across the river with all of their belongings. The girl was an only child and had no comrades to help her enter life. Such a situation—for instance, when the parents marry late or have no children for a long time—often brings on tragic difficulties. By taking the skull to her room, the girl calls forth hostile reactions from her surroundings; she arouses the fear and hatred of her parents. An animus to which the woman is not related often attracts hostility (aimed at the woman) without her suspecting the reason. The negative reactions of other people are a sign that an essential part of her personality has not been realized by her. The environment seeks to irritate and prod her, as it were, into recognizing what she lacks.

When the girl is forsaken, she reproaches the skull for her loneliness. The skull tells her to gather faggots, make a big fire, and throw him on it; in that way he will acquire a body.

Fire generally represents emotion and passion, which can either burn one up or spread light. Sacrifices are burned in order to dissolve the physical part so that the image or essence may rise with the smoke to the gods. When, however, a "spirit creature" is burned, the burning confers a body upon it. Passion compels one to sacrifice a too-independent, too-intellectual attitude, and passion enables one to realize the spirit. When one undergoes passionate suffering, the spirit is no longer an idea but is experienced as psychic reality. Therefore the skull implores the girl to throw him into the fire. "Otherwise," he says to her, "we are both suffering in vain." One must fight suffering with suffering—with the acceptance of suffering. Torturing the skull in the fire means to fight fire with fire and to repay the torment she has suffered from him. The animus awakens passion in a woman. His plans, purposes, and whims stir up self-doubt within her and cause her to drag her feminine, passive nature out into the world and to expose herself to the resistance of the outer world. Then, when a woman has been successful in a man's world, it means acute suffering to narrow down the scope of her activities, or to give them up altogether, in order to become more feminine again.

In alchemy, fire frequently symbolizes one's participation in the work and is equated with the passion one gives to the different stages of the alchemical process.

The skull tells the girl that she must cover her eyes and be sure not to look at the burning. Here again is the motif of the danger of too-early enlightenment. One must not grasp intellectually all that happens in the psyche, by no means always define and categorize all inner happenings; often one must curb one's curiosity and simply wait. Only a strong person, however, is able to control his or her impatience and let the interplay go on without looking, whereas a weaker consciousness wants to have the dream interpreted at once because it is so afraid of the uncertainty and the darkness of the situation. The girl has to wait in the darkness while she listens to the roar of the flames and the confusion of horses and men rushing past. Being terrified yet remaining firm and untouched by panic denotes a strength beyond hope and despair. But many cannot wait and prefer sudden decisions. In this way they disturb their fate and its inscrutable working. In the end there stands before the girl a man robed in animal skins, attended by a group of people and animals. He is very rich and she becomes his wife, with the result that she now has a powerful positive animus and much joy in life. Later her parents return to visit her, and she kills them by giving them splintered marrow bones—which is more than they can swallow.

THE MOTIF OF RELATIONSHIP

There are many tales whose leading characters can be interpreted as representing either the anima or the animus. These tales depict the human patterns of relationship: the processes that take place between man and woman or the fundamental facts of the psyche beyond the masculine and feminine differences. Most tales of mutual redemption are of this type.

In such tales, children often have the leading roles—for instance, "Hänsel and Gretel." Because children are relatively undifferentiated both sexually and psychically, they are much closer to the hermaphroditic original being. The child is thus an apt symbol of the Self—of an inner future totality and, at the same time, of undeveloped facets of one's individuality. The child signifies a piece of innocence and wonder surviving in us from the remote past, both that part of our personal childishness which has been bypassed and the new, early form of the future individuality. Seen in this light, the saying "The child is father to the man" has deeper significance.

These tales are not concerned with human and personal factors but with the development of the archetypes; they show the ways in which the archetypes are related to one another within the collective unconscious.

There is a fairy tale in which the coming together of the masculine and feminine psyches is presented from the angle of the unconscious; however, as the reader will see, the reality of the feminine psyche is more clearly revealed than that of the masculine psyche.

The White Bride and the Black Bride

Once upon a time, God appeared as a poor man to a woman, her daughter, and her stepdaughter, and asked them to tell him the way to the village. The woman and her daughter scorned him, but the stepdaughter offered to show him the way. In return God caused the woman and her daughter to become black and ugly and conferred upon the stepdaughter three blessings: very great beauty, an inexhaustible purse of money, and the kingdom of heaven when she should die.

The stepdaughter's brother, Reginer, who was the king's coachman, thought his sister so beautiful that he painted her portrait and gazed at it daily. One day the king heard about the portrait and asked to see it, and because of her overwhelming beauty he fell in love with the sister of Reginer and ordered the coachman to fetch her. Brother and sister rode to the king, together with the black stepmother and stepsister. On the way the jealous stepmother pushed her beautiful stepdaughter into the river, an act for which Reginer was held responsible, and at the order of the king he was thrown into a snakepit. By means of her black arts the stepmother duped the king into marrying her boundlessly ugly daughter.

The stepdaughter was not drowned, however. She turned into a white duck, which for three nights appeared to the king's kitchen boy and talked with him. The kitchen boy reported this to the king, who came on the fourth night and beheaded the duck, who then instantly changed back into her most beautiful self. She then told the king about the stepmother's perfidy, and the king punished the witch and her black daughter mercilessly, rescued Reginer from the snakepit, and married the bride.[54]

The woman, her daughter and her stepdaughter can be regarded as a triad representing the feminine psyche. The woman would represent the conscious attitude, while the genuine daughter, who is negative, represents the shadow, and Reginer, the stepbrother, stands for the animus. The stepdaughter is the fourth, and she represents the true inner nature and source of renewal within the feminine psyche. However, she can reach fulfillment only when she gets in touch with the discerning Logos principle personified by the king.

The king does not belong to a foursome, but he is one of three masculine figures, the other two being the coachman, who makes the connection with the anima, and the kitchen boy, who leads him to the revelation of the inner situation.

God appears to the first triad of the woman and her two daughters and rewards the one who shows him the way, but the woman and her daughter are cursed and made black; that is, they are covered over by the veil of unconsciousness. Their sin was that they refused to show God the way, and this suggests that God needs man to help him. He asks man to be the instrument for reaching higher consciousness. In the mystical sense this means that the human psyche is the place where God can become conscious.

Because the two women fail at this task, they forfeit their

human essence and become witches. Falling under the dark veil of unconsciousness, they step out of their role as representatives of female consciousness, which they had at the tale's beginning, and play the role of the negative anima. When this happens one cannot discriminate between an unconscious woman and the anima of a man. Psychologically there is no distinction. A woman who is lost in the sea of the unconscious is vague in herself and has neither critical understanding nor much will. Such an undefined woman easily plays the role of the anima for men. Indeed, the more unconscious she is, the better she can play the anima role. It is for this reason that some women are reluctant to become conscious; if they do, they lose the ability to be the witch-anima and thus lose their power over men. Similarly, a man who is drowned in the unconscious behaves like the animus of a woman. A possessed man—Hitler, for example—has all the animus traits; he is carried away by every emotion, is full of unconsidered opinions, and expresses himself sloppily and didactically, often in an emotional uproar.

The beautiful white bride is pushed into the water and swims away in the form of a white duck, while Reginer, the animus whose task it was to lead her to the king, the real contact with the Logos, is thrown into a snakepit. But the lowly shadow of the king, the kitchen boy, is instrumental in bringing out the truth.

When the king beheads the duck, she again turns into a beautiful woman. If a psychic content is not recognized in the human realm, it regresses into the instinctual realm, as we saw in the case of Snati-Snati. After the witch and her daughter have been destroyed, a mandala of four persons emerges: the king, the white bride, Reginer freed from the pit, and the kitchen boy.

While there is much more that one could say about this story, I cite it only to show how a factor which represents the consciousness of a woman can at the same time be identified with the negative anima of a man.

Many tales light up different aspects, yet at the same time contain similar motifs such as witches, stepmothers, and kings, and always a similar process, the same energic way of proceeding, and this gives us a hint. The fact that the threads running through the tales all follow the same direction—so that several tales can be linked up into a circular chain of rings of tales, each amplifying the other—suggests that the order they refer to is a fundamental one. It is my feeling that when fairy tales are brought together in clusters and interpreted in relation to one another, they represent at bottom one transcendental archetypal arrangement.

There is a type of fairy tale which especially focuses on the problem of encounters with the Self. Such fairy tales revolve around the theme of surmounting great difficulties to reach a treasure. But indirectly, the Self makes an appearance in nearly all fairy tales. For example, it is touched upon in the toad's ring in "The Three Feathers"; in the name Ring, which is the name of the king's son in the Snati-Snati story; and in the prickly fish on the altar of the mountain spirit. Indeed, the hard-to-attain treasure is often present in the guise of simple things. When one is interpreting fairy tales, it pays to always keep an eye open for this central motif.

In the same way that a crystal may be illuminated from its various sides, so each kind of tale presents certain aspects and necessarily obscures others. For instance, in one tale certain archetypes can be seen particularly clearly, while in another story other archetypes emerge. And there are groups of tales, all of which refer to the same configuration of archetypes.

It is tempting to try to create an abstract model of the general structure of the collective unconscious, representing it as a crystal, in itself one and the same but manifested in ten thousand different fairy tales. However, I do not believe this to be possible because I assume that we are dealing with a transcendental order similar to the atom, which physicists say cannot be described as it is in itself because three-dimensional models inevitably distort it. While schemata can be invaluable, the four-dimensional event forever eludes our grasp.

Although the inner order refuses to be schematized, we can nevertheless obtain hints of that order by observing that all the different tales circumambulate one and the same content—the Self.

NOTES

—— ❧❧❧❧❧❧ ——

1. Lucius Apuleius, *The Golden Ass,* trans. William Adlington, 1566; revised by S. Gaselee (Cambridge: Harvard University Press, Loeb Classical Library, 1915).
2. Fr. Max Schmidt, *The Primitive Races of Mankind* (London, Calcutta & Sydney: George G. Harrag & Co., 1926).
3. Cf. L. W. von Bülow, *Die Geheimsprache der Märchen,* or P. L. Stauff, *Märchendeutungen,* 1914.
4. Theodor Benfey, *Kleinere Schriften zur Märchenforschung* (Berlin, 1894).
5. Antti Aarne, *Types of Folk Tales* (Helsinki, 1961).
6. Ludwig Laistner, *Das Rätsel der Sphinx* (Berlin, 1889).
7. Adolf Bastian, *Beiträge zur vergleichenden Psychologie* (Berlin, 1868).
8. Georg Jakob, *Märchen und Traum* (Hannover, 1923).
9. Stith Thompson, *Motif Index of Folk Literature* (Bloomington: Indiana University Studies, 1932–1936).
10. See, for instance, the work of Max Lüthi, *Das europäische Volksmärchen* (Bern, 1947).
11. Julius Schwabe, *Archetyp und Tierkreis.* Mircea Eliade, *Myth and Reality,* trans. Willard R. Trask (New York: Harper & Row, 1963), and *The Myth of the Eternal Return,* trans. Willard R. Trask (Princeton, N.J.: Princeton University Press, Bollingen Series XLVI, 1974).
12. C. G. Jung, "Approaching the Unconscious," in *Man and His Symbols* (New York: Doubleday & Co., 1969).
13. Max Lüthi, "Die Gabe im Märchen und in der Sage." Inaugural dissertation, Bern, 1943.
14. *Schweiz. Zeitschrift für Volkskunde,* 1937.
15. Cf. Paul Kugler, "Remarques sur les rapports de la théorie des archétypes et du structuralisme," *Cahier de Psychologie Jungienne,* no. 29 (1981); 35–47.
16. *Die Märchen der Weltliteratur* (Tales of World Literature) (Jena: Diederichs Verlag), a multivolume series.
17. Edward B. Tylor, *Primitive Culture* (London, 1981).
18. John G. Niehardt, ed., *Black Elk Speaks: Being the Life Story of a Holy Man of the Oglala Sioux* (New York: William Morrow Co., 1932).

19. Knud Rasmussen, *Die Gabe des Adlers* (Frankfurt am Main: Societäts Verlag, 1937).

20. R. M. Berndt, *Kunapipi* (Melbourne: Cheshire, 1951).

21. Laurens van der Post, *The Heart of the Hunter* (London: Hogarth Press, 1961).

22. *The Complete Grimm's Fairy Tales* (New York: Pantheon Books, 1972), p. 319.

23. J. Bolte and G. Polívka, *Anmerkungen zu den Kinder- und Hausmärchen der Brüder Grimm,* 5 vols. (Leipzig, 1913–1927). See vol. 3, p. 30.

24. C. G. Jung, *Collected Works,* vol. 14, trans. R. F. C. Hull (Princeton, N.J.: Princeton University Press, Bollingen Series XX, 1970).

25. Hanns Bächtold-Stäubli, *Handwörterbuch des deutschen Aberglaubens* (Berlin & Leipzig: W. de Gruyter & Co., 1930–1931).

26. C. G. Jung, *Collected Works,* vol. 11, *Psychology and Religion West and East,* chap. 2.

27. C. G. Jung, *Collected Works,* vol. 18, chap. 3.

28. *Die Märchen der Weltliteratur: Russische Volksmärchen,* no. 5 (1921).

29. This version, which appears under the title "Snati-Snati," is taken from Adeline Ritterhaus, *Die neuisländischen Volkmärchen* (Halle, A. S., 1902).

30. For other parallels, see Carl Pschmadt, "Die Sage von der verfolgten Hinde," dissertation, Greifswald, 1911.

31. C. G. Jung, *Collected Works,* vol. 8, *The Structure and Dynamics of the Psyche.*

32. *Die Märchen der Weltliteratur: Deutsche Märchen seit Grimm* (1922), p. 237.

33. *Die Märchen der Weltliteratur: Nordische Märchen* (1915), p. 22.

34. Ibid., p. 194.

35. *Die Märchen der Weltliteratur: Südamerika indianische Märchen,* no. 76 (1921), p. 206.

36. See "Berg," in *Handwörterbuch des deutschen Aberglaubens.*

37. C. G. Jung, *Collected Works,* vol. 12, *Psychology and Alchemy,* and vol. 13, *Alchemical Studies.*

38. For a discussion of the horse as a symbol, see C. G. Jung, *Collected Works,* vol. 5, *Symbols of Transformation,* paras. 421–428 and 657–659.

39. See C. G. Jung, *Collected Works,* vol. 11, *Psychology and Religion West and East,* chap. 3, "Transformation Symbolism in the Mass."

40. Apuleius, *The Golden Ass.*

41. Mrs. Rhys David, "Zur Geschichte des Rad Symbols," Eranos Jahrbuch (Zurich: Rascher, 1934).

42. See *Handbuch des deutschen Aberglaubens.*

43. *Die Märchen der Weltliteratur: Nordische Volksmärchen* (1915), vol. 11, no. 32, "Zottelhaube."

44. See C. G. Jung, *Collected Works,* vol. 16, *The Practice of Psychotherapy,* part 2, sec. 3, "The Psychology of the Transference."

45. *Grimm's Fairy Tales* (London: Routledge, 1948), p. 244.

46. *Die Märchen der Weltliteratur: Französische Volkmärchen*, no. 32 (1923).

47. Ibid., *Zigeunermärchen*, no. 31 (1926).

48. Ibid., *Märchen aus Turkestan und Tibet*, no. 9 (1923).

49. Ibid., *Balkanmärchen*, no. 12 (1919).

50. See C. G. Jung, *Collected Works*, vol. 10, *Civilization in Transition*, chap. 3, "Wotan."

51. *Die Märchen der Weltliteratur: Märchen aus Sibirien* (1940), p. 81.

52. Ibid., p. 121.

53. Cf. Sartori, "Der Schuh im Volksglauben," *Zeitschrift für Volkskunde* (1894), pp. 41, 148, and 282.

54. *Grimm's Fairy Tales*, p. 608.

INDEX

C. G. Jung Foundation Books

Absent Fathers, Lost Sons: The Search for Masculine Identity, by Guy Corneau

Alchemical Active Imagination, by Marie-Louise von Franz

*Archetypal Dimensions of the Psyche, by Marie-Louise von Franz

Creation Myths, revised edition, by Marie-Louise von Franz

Depth Psychology and a New Ethic, by Erich Neumann

Dreams, by Marie-Louise von Franz. Foreword by Robert Hinshaw

Ego and Archetype: Individuation and the Religious Function of the Psyche, by Edward F. Edinger

The Feminine in Fairy Tales, revised edition, by Marie-Louise von Franz

From Freud to Jung: A Comparative Study of the Psychology of the Unconscious, by Liliane Frey-Rohn

The Golden Ass of Apuleius: The Liberation of the Feminine in Man, by Marie-Louise von Franz

A Guided Tour of the Collected Works of C. G. Jung, by Robert H. Hopcke

Individuation in Fairy Tales, revised edition, by Marie-Louise von Franz

The Inner Child in Dreams, by Kathrin Asper. Translated by Sharon E. Rooks

The Interpretation of Fairy Tales, revised edition, by Marie-Louise von Franz

Knowing Woman: A Feminine Psychology, by Irene Claremont de Castillejo

Masculinity: Identity, Conflict, and Transformation, by Warren Steinberg

Old Wise Woman: A Study of the Active Imagination, by Rix Weaver

Psyche and Matter, by Marie-Louise von Franz. Foreword by Robert Hinshaw

Psychotherapy, by Marie-Louise von Franz

Shadow and Evil in Fairy Tales, revised edition, by Marie-Louise von Franz

Transforming Sexuality: The Archetypal World of Anima and Animus, by Ann Belford Ulanov and Barry Ulanov

*Published in association with Daimon Verlag, Einsiedeln, Switzerland.